Make It Your BUSINESS

A MEMOIR ABOUT POSSIBILITIES

Dare to Climb the Ladder of Leadership

Sylvia M. Montero

PRAISE FOR
Make It Your Business

"Sylvia Montero is an amazing woman. I feel fortunate to count her as a colleague and friend. Her story is inspirational. In this book Sylvia tells how she rose from the poverty of the little house on stilts on a sugar cane plantation in Puerto Rico to being the senior Human Resources Officer at Pfizer Inc, the world's largest pharmaceutical company. More important, she provides valuable inspiration and life and career success advice for young people coping with difficult circumstances. This book is a must read – for its inspirational story and it's common sense life and career success advice."

  – *Bud Bilanich, The Common Sense Guy, Denver, Colorado*

"Sylvia Montero's book is a great source book for anyone climbing the corporate ladder – and a great read for anyone who believes in the American Dream. Ms. Montero has lived that Dream, and the lessons she learned along the way can teach us all about the meaning of success in the truest sense. I loved it!"

  – *Andrew G. Celli, Jr., Emery, Celli, Brinckerhoff & Abady, LLP, New York*

"An amazing story of the voyage from the depths of poverty to the pinnacle of success. Commitment, dedication and perseverance highlight the remarkable courage and determination that was the foundation of this motivational life story. As a friend and business colleague it was indeed inspirational to watch Sylvia's strengths and leadership qualities demonstrated day in and day out as she climbed the ladder of success. A must read for all who are pursuing the American Dream"

> – *Brian W. Barrett, Vice President, Pfizer Inc. (retired), New York*

"Sylvia Montero's wonderful book is full of lessons for those seeking to live their dreams in their personal and professional lives. Her rise in the corporate world from a humble background offers real-world advice into what it takes to be successful. She is honest about the challenges she faced and helpful in sharing what she learned from both her successes and setbacks. Her book provides inspiration and guidance to young men and women as they make their way in the world."

> – *Robert B. Shaw, Management Consultant & Author,*
> *Princeton, New Jersey*

"A best in class role model of a woman who has had a phenomenal journey of success to the very top of leadership. A book that will touch the hearts of readers and from which everyone will benefit, as business leaders and as human beings. Having had the privilege of working with her I can include myself among the many leaders who were touched by her magic and helped maximize their potential. A must read for our growing number of minorities striving to succeed in business."

> – *Pedro Lichtinger, President and CEO, Optimer Pharmaceuticals,*
> *San Diego, California*

"A touching and inspiring story of struggles and triumphs. Sylvia's story will resonate with wise Latinas and others who find that we can convert our challenges into opportunities."

> – *Margarita Rosa, Executive Director, Grand Street Settlement,*
> *New York*

DEDICATION

For my grandchildren,
Kenny and Miranda.

In honor of my parents,
Eligia Montero (1928 – Present)
And
Cruz Montero (1922 – 2006)

To the Diversity +
Inclusion Council,
With best wishes
for the success of
the work that you
do   Sylvia
Oct 4, 2011

CONTENTS

ACKNOWLEDGEMENTS

Thank you

*"You have a story to tell. You ought to write a book,
and if you decide to do so, I will help you."*

Bud Bilanich made this generous offer over dinner just days after I retired. A year later I took him up on it. Bud is the 'Common Sense Guy,' a success coach, motivational speaker, author, blogger and my friend. True to his goal to "help as many people as I can to create the successful lives and careers they want and deserve," Bud spent many hours on the phone helping me think through my themes, sharing his own life experiences and professional knowledge. For two years, Bud gave selflessly of his talent and skills so that my story will reach a broader audience who might be helped by it. Why? Because that is the type of guy he is. I encourage you to meet this extraordinary man at www.budbilanich.com. Bud, with my deepest gratitude.

I am grateful to my parents, Cruz and Eligia Montero, for the heroism of their lives; for their fierce devotion to their five children; for their tough love; for never giving up. I regret that my father is not alive to read this, but I believe he knew my feelings. Thankfully, Mom was able to add her memories and will read the book in its Spanish translation.

Thanks to my siblings—Miriam, Elba, Rod and Wally—who, having shared the same experiences growing up, made sure that my memories were true and accurate. Special thanks to Miriam for also applying her teacher's red pen to every detail of my manuscript and for coming up with the title of the book.

Thanks to my son, Ken, for his feedback and for that wonderful three-way discussion with Bud and me, sharing his perspective growing up with a single working Mom.

I must also thank many colleagues and friends who took the time to read my manuscript and provided precious feedback, particularly Don and Sandy, Brian, Monta, Jim and Pat, Mark and Patricia, Maria M., Hannah, Robert, Joe, the Smith family, Cathy, Sharon, Neil and Pedro, among others.

Special thanks to my editor and collaborator, Yosef Baskin, for "helping my more-tame written voice match my more-fiery in-person voice."

I am grateful to my husband O.B., who always read the earliest draft of each chapter. For his time and patience, his love of the English language, his empathy and broad perspective, thank you.

Finally, I am indebted to the many mentors and sponsors who guided a young girl from the little house on stilts to the Boardroom.

Part One

Prologue

The Boardroom

I waited outside the beautifully polished, double wooden doors on the executive floor. Waiting to be called in by the Board of Pfizer Inc., I breathed deeply taking it all in, not wanting to forget any detail of this incredible moment. To make sure of being calm and at my best, I had gone to the gym that morning just like every weekday. I wore one of my best colors—a bright blue knit jacket over a black ankle-length skirt. I wanted to look my personal best: self-assured, positive and glowing.

Suddenly the doors opened and the Secretary of the Board beckoned me into the room. I sprung up and followed her into the traditional boardroom. A full 50% of the room was taken up by a massive conference table. Around it were the members of the Board of Pfizer Inc. plus my former boss John LaMattina, President of the Research & Development Group. I was announced as I entered the room, "Ladies and Gentlemen of the Board, Ms. Sylvia Montero, Senior Vice President of Human Resources, Pfizer Inc." The CEO of Pfizer Inc, Hank McKinnell, and the entire Board stood as one and applauded. As the Secretary steered me around the table, one by one each Board member shook my hand and congratulated me. I concentrated intently on making eye contact with each one, to remember each pair of eyes and each strong handshake. John LaMattina hugged me with pride in his eyes. I continued the round aware of the historical significance of my appointment to the highest H.R. position in this remarkable company.

Twenty six years earlier, as a candidate for an entry-level H.R. position in Pfizer, Puerto Rico, I had flown to New York to interview with Don Lum, then head of Human Resources for Pfizer Inc. He asked me what my career goal was, and I didn't hesitate to answer "Your job." Although he seemed slightly surprised by my answer, he smiled and graciously wished me the best.

Don was my predecessor five times removed and I felt his presence in the room as I concluded my walk around the huge table. There was pageantry to the process that linked every person in that room to their own predecessors many times removed.

I walked out of the room the first Hispanic appointed to the top H.R. position of Pfizer Inc., the largest pharmaceutical company in the world. Despite the earlier, over-confident remark to Don Lum, I never imagined myself actually in the office. This moment was truly far beyond my dreams.

I thought about the road that led me to the boardroom and I could not contain a smile of pride as I remembered the beginning …

Part Two
The Story

Innocent Happiness

I am born in Cabo Rojo, southwestern Puerto Rico, a most anxiously awaited daughter. After the birth of two boys, *Mamita* prays to the Virgin of Miracles, *La Milagrosa*, for a girl that she promised to name Milagros—therefore my name, Silvia Milagros Montero. (In Puerto Rico I add Cáceres, Mamita's maiden name.) In fact, she prays so hard that she gets three girls: Elba and Miriam follow soon after. By my third birthday, there are five of us, with two older brothers and two younger sisters. Mamita is 24 years old, and *Papito*, 30.

We live in a little wooden house on stilts. No plumbing and no electricity. The outhouse and bathhouse are towards the back. Tropical fruit trees grow all around our little house. It's a tiny four-room house, but we are comfortable in it. The house is located in the middle of the sugar cane plantation where Papito works. We don't own it, of course. It was previously used to house single men who worked the plantation. But when our parents got married, the foreman generously let them live in it. They must have not wanted to lose Papito's work, because he's an excellent worker.

Our memories of those young years are happy ones. In Puerto Rico the sun shines hot, and to cool off, we crawl under the house and play in the shaded soil. We're not afraid of the worms that also find 'under the house' a better place to be. But when it rains, it rains. What a pleasure when we run in the rain! The sound of rain on the zinc roof is a lullaby; I love to hear the sound of rain on metal.

Papito pumps water from the nearby well into two buckets that hang from the ends of a yoke around his neck and shoulders. The water is poured into a big barrel in the kitchen, and from there we scoop out water for all of our needs: to cook, to drink, to bathe, to wash dishes. A metal sheet covers the barrel to keep out the bugs and dust. The sink is a square metal box with a hole in the middle, attached to the outside of the kitchen window. A ditch carries the dirty dishwater away from the house.

Papito's parents, *Abuelo* and *Abuela*, live a little further up the dirt road past the well. We often walk to their house for family gatherings and usually end the day praying the rosary. We love to climb on top of the big rock in front of their house. It's big enough for many of us to climb on at the same time, and the older cousins tell many stories. We all learn that dwarfs, goblins, elves and other scary monsters live under that rock. For the walk back, Papito always carries a flashlight to light our way and also to make sure that we don't step on a centipede—the bite is very painful. The clear night sky is filled to capacity with millions of stars. The nights are beyond noisy because of the ever-present crickets. But distinct and clear through the loud crickets, we hear the unmistakable music of the *coquí*, a tiny tree frog with a big voice.

The nearest 'village' is within walking distance. It's called 'Delicias Branch,' the U.S. postal address. Our uncle, *Tío* Alejandro and his family live there. He has two daughters who are my playmates along with my siblings and the foreman's daughters. The one-room school house for first, second and third grades is a little beyond Tío's house. *Tía* Elena is the cook. I try to use this relationship to avoid eating boiled pumpkin, but it's no use; I still have to eat it. For morning break we get milk made from powder. The glasses are put out in the sun so the milk is warm by morning break. My brother, Radames, doesn't like warm milk, so he cajoles me into drinking his portion as well.

We are excellent students. Our parents drill into us the importance of education and doing well in school. Papito went to school until fifth grade and Mamita until third, both dropping out to help support their families. Later, as a teenager, Papito completed another three years of school in the evenings.

When the sun sets, we use mostly candles to light the house. We own one hurricane lamp that is used to light the living room. Once, Waldemar, the eldest, complains of a headache, and Mamita rubs some medicine on his head. The medicine contained alcohol, so when *Waldy* got too close to a candle, his head catches fire. What a scramble to put out the fire—Papito threw himself around Waldy, smothered the fire with his body and then had to figure out how to get him to the hospital in town. Luckily a distant neighbor owned a car. Waldy escaped with minor burns, but I always remember the smell of burning hair.

We use mosquito netting to cover our beds. Mosquitoes are big and they are many, and if one gets into bed with us, it's a challenge to find it. The mosquito net is a safe and comforting barrier between us and the outside world.

Christmas is a holy day but Three Kings Day is the fun day. Before bed on the night of January 5th, we put out grass and water for the camels to eat when the Magi come with gifts. I have a happy memory of waking up one morning to something solid and cool on my face—a creamy ceramic face with blue eyes that open and close, my first doll. Mom is so happy that I retain this memory, as a store -bought doll must have required a special sacrifice. Without many store-bought toys, we are creative in our games. Radames imitates Papito's work by using empty cans to simulate the oxcarts that carry sugar cane to the loading crane. A piece of string looped over the lowest branch of the avocado tree in the front yard becomes the crane that moves bundles of sugar cane from the cart to the truck.

A little creek flows behind our house. We like to fish using a string with a bent pin at the end. We catch small eels, and sometimes we enjoy the tiny morsels roasted over an open fire.

We raise or grow a lot of our food. Abuelo also works on the sugarcane plantation, and so he and Abuela are allowed to use part of the land for agriculture. Papito and Tío Alejandro help to seed and till the land, sharing in its produce: root vegetables such as yucca, yautía and ñame. They also plant banana, plantain, beans, black eye peas and pigeon peas. Our parents raise chickens for meat and eggs and, of course, the annual pig. We eat every part of the pig in all sorts of delicious preparations, the most exotic of which is the *morsilla*, a blood sausage made out of the intestines. Tia Juana is the best pig 'chef' in the family. She removes and meticulously cleans the intestines. Then she seasons the blood with local spices—garlic, onion, cilantro, peppers, oregano, pours it into the intestines, ties both ends and fries the sausage.

Our staple is rice and beans prepared in a variety of different ways. Waldy and Radames trap land crabs using an empty metal cracker box. When they are successful we enjoy crab meat, a special treat. Sometimes we get permission to go into a nearby coffee plantation to pick coffee beans. I use my skirt to form a bucket and when it's full I empty the beans into the larger sack. Our parents dry the coffee beans in the sun and roast and grind it. This saves them money they would have had to spend to buy ground coffee. Our diet is supplemented by the fruit of many tropical trees—coconut, avocado, starchy breadfruit, mango, papaya, sweet and sour oranges, tart soursop, grapefruit, bittersweet tamarind and many more.

Papito goes to the *bodega* for additional groceries. He has to spend money to buy the things we can't grow or raise, such as rice and powdered milk. Abuelo stops by our house every week on his way back from the bodega and he always has a treat for us—cupcakes or some sweet. It must be a sacrifice for him to spend even the few pennies those treats cost. We have priceless memories of the excitement waiting for him to stop by.

Papito earns $15 to $20 a week based on how many rows of sugar cane he seeds, cultivates or cuts. It's a blessing that he doesn't have to pay to live in the house. Later my father is promoted to operate the crane from the motor house and his wages are increased to $30 dollars a week. Mamita helps by stitching gloves, piece work from a local factory. She earns $2.35 or $3.75 a dozen according to the style of glove. June through September is *tiempo muerto*, dead time on the plantation, and that means no work for Papito and no income. So Mamita teaches Papito how to stitch gloves and they both stitch late into the evening. It still isn't enough for our groceries, so they have to take the groceries on credit. Papito repays the bodega owner when he starts working again. It is almost impossible to catch up. One day the glove factory moves to the Philippines, and there is no more supplementary income. Our parents are afraid they can't feed their children. That's when they decide that Papito will move stateside as a migrant farm worker. And just like that, our lives are turned upside down.

Nueva York
A Wondrous Place

*N*ueva York was a wondrous place in our minds. We looked
forward to fairy tale beauty and magical things. The buildings would be
silvery with beautiful balconies. The wide streets would be lined with
trees and flowers, full of beautiful cars. Work was plentiful and
everybody was rich. These perceptions had been formed by listening to
the stories of those who were fortunate enough to return for visits.

Some of Mamita's family had already made the transition to Nueva
York. Mamita's brother, Julio, had joined the army and from there he
stayed in Nueva York. This young, handsome and uniformed uncle
added to the stories of Nueva York that formed our expectations of the
city that was to be our new home. Also in Nueva York were Mamá (our
maternal grandmother), Tía Carmen and Domingo ('Mingo'), Mamita's
siblings. We didn't call Julio and Mingo *Tío* because they were just boys
when we were born. They persuaded Papito to stay in Nueva York and
his niece, Julia, helped him find a job in the costume jewelry factory
where she worked. There he earned the minimum wage, $1.00 an hour,

a lot more than he made on the plantation. He missed us terribly, and within a month, on July 4, 1957, we were on our way to Nueva York.

The flight cost $186 for all six of us, mostly borrowed from the family in Nueva York, except for $35 that Mamita got from selling what little furniture we had. Our uncle, Julio, sent new dresses for the three girls; the boys wore their 'good' school clothes. The three-hour trip by public car, from southwest Puerto Rico through the curvy roads of the inner island to San Juan in the northeast, cost $15. Tío Alejandro and Tía Elena accompanied us to the airport so, aside from the driver, there were nine of us crammed like sardines, with the youngest ones on laps. The five children were ages four to ten; I was seven.

The overnight flight on a propeller plane left at 11:30 p.m. and arrived early next morning. Terrified, we remained frozen to our seats for the entire trip. We must have looked frightened, because the stewardesses seemed to hover over us more than other passengers. Mamita didn't dare leave her seat and another passenger helped Radames to the lavatory. The girls were dolled up in our new dresses with stiff petticoats that popped in the air when we sat down. For the big event, Tía Elena had given us short hair cuts easy to groom. The ups and downs of the plane made me motion sick.

We were very happy to land at Idlewild Airport (later renamed John F. Kennedy International Airport). However, the drive from the airport to our apartment gave us our first real impressions of Nueva York and what a disappointment it was. We drove through claustrophobic 'tunnels' formed by tall buildings on either side. We stared wide-eyed as our expectation of fairytale beauty was replaced by soot-blackened buildings with corroded fire escapes.

For the first three months we lived in a furnished room on Manhattan's West 78th Street, not far from the Museum of Natural History. When we got to the one-room apartment that was to be our home, we were disappointed that there was no 'under the house' to play in, and we missed the outdoors. Mamita was afraid to let us go outside to play and we had to avoid the landlord so he wouldn't find out just how many of us—seven—were living in one room. Inevitably, he did find out and we were asked to leave. We moved to a tenement apartment in the Lower East Side near Tía Carmen's apartment. The apartment was across the street from the neighborhood park and the pool. Finally, the boys were able to go out and play while Mamita watched from the window. The girls were always much more closely supervised. The apartment was very cold. The building had no boiler and Mamita was afraid to light the gas heater for fear of a fire. However, we were glad to have more space: two bedrooms, the kitchen and a small living room. Waldy and Radamés shared a bed in one room; our parents and the girls slept in the other room. I slept with Elba and Miriam in one bed and our parents had the other bed.

Our parents had paid the previous occupant for his meager furniture, and we quickly discovered that the beds were infested with bed bugs. The entire building was infested with cockroaches and no level of cleanliness inside the apartment kept them out. Mamita was beside herself. Despite the country soil we grew up in, this was the first time that we lived in such dirty conditions. We were careful to check our coats for cockroaches before leaving the house. I got used to sleeping on my side with a corner of the blanket draped over my exposed ear because I was afraid that a cockroach would crawl into my ear. I had that habit for many years even after I no longer had to worry about cockroaches.

We got sick right away. In Puerto Rico we had been vaccinated only for Small Pox, so in Nueva York we came down with all the childhood diseases. Who knows how our parents handled five children with the Mumps, the Chicken Pox and the Measles one after another; the boys also got Whooping Cough; Miriam, the youngest, developed Asthma; and, of course, we caught one cold after another. Our uncle, Julio, the only family member with a car, often rushed one of us to the hospital wrapped in a blanket. I still remember my embarrassment because my handsome, young uncle could see my bare bottom when the nurse gave me a shot of penicillin.

We were enrolled in the local grammar school, PS-4. Miriam (age 5) and Elba (age 6) started kindergarten and first grade, respectively. This was their first school experience because there was no kindergarten in our country schoolhouse. Radamés (age 9) and I (age 8) were mortified we had to repeat second and third grades, respectively. Mamita pleaded with the school authorities to allow Waldy (age 11), her eldest, to continue on to the next grade. Waldy had been an A student in Puerto Rico with excellent prospects for a scholarship. She must have been very convincing, because they placed him in fifth grade.

The first year of school was extremely difficult, especially English and Social Studies. We learned English through total immersion; more than half the time we didn't know what the teachers were saying even though they would speak more slowly to us. They told us not to speak Spanish at home, an impossible expectation because our parents didn't speak English. We wanted to learn English quickly so that we would fit in: Waldy borrowed reading books from the lower grades so that he could read them at home at his own pace; we sat next to other Spanish-speaking kids who could help us out. We all remember embarrassing moments when a mispronunciation or awkward sentence structure would get a laugh from the kids.

But we built up our vocabulary and worked hard to eliminate the accent. Some sounds were more difficult than others. We had trouble with the long and short 'e' sounds, the 'th' sounds, the American 'r', the 't' that sounded like 'r', the 'ch' and 'sch' that were pronounced 'k', etc. Yet, the transition from not speaking English to speaking it was so quick for me that I don't really remember the process in between.

Miriam was so frequently sick that our parents decided to pull her out of kindergarten. Not knowing the rules and thinking that kindergarten was optional, they just stopped sending her to school. One day an intimidating social worker came to our apartment asking why Miriam wasn't in school. Terrified, Mamita asked a neighbor to translate and the social worker saw first-hand our living situation. The $22 weekly rent depleted Papito's $40 pay check. After tax deductions and tokens for the subway, he was left with $10 a week for his family of seven. Miriam was allowed to stay home and we received an emergency check for $129. That's how we ended up on Welfare and placed on a priority list for subsidized public housing.

Almost two years to the day after arriving in Nueva York, we moved to a five-room apartment in the newly built projects near the FDR Drive and the Williamsburg Bridge to Brooklyn. We were so happy because it seemed like a palace to us: my sisters and I had our own room, the boys another and our parents finally had a private room. We were comfortable and warm, and we could control the roaches. With the security of Papito's job, the welfare check and the extra food, our parents finally felt that they could feed us. Elba and Miriam were delighted they didn't always have to wear my hand-me-downs. It was then that our parents decided we would stay in Nueva York. Before that, Mamita had yearned for the familiarity and cleanliness of our little house in Puerto Rico, which the plantation foreman kept unoccupied for three years in case we decided to go back.

Mamita was fanatical about cleaning our apartment, with full power over a small army of six to assist her in that task. On Saturday mornings we each did our chores under her critical eye. The boys cleaned the windows; the girls washed and ironed. With no washing machine and little money to spend on laundromats, we washed clothes and bedding by hand in the deep kitchen sink. And we all had our turn wiping fingerprints and smudges off the grayish-white walls. Papito completed the process by sweeping and mopping the floor after everything else was spotless. Only then could we think of doing something that was fun.

Five years later, we were offered an apartment in a new public housing nearby. We couldn't believe the mansion we moved into. With four bedrooms, I got my own room!

Raising and Educating Puerto Rican Children

Welfare. It was our big family secret. Mamita and Papito were embarrassed they couldn't support their family independently, so we didn't volunteer that information to family or friends. The process itself was also very humiliating. We called the social worker, always a man, *El investigador*—the probing questions and technique of scanning the apartment told us all he was investigating. He usually showed up during the day—no appointments—so Mamita had to get a neighbor to interpret. One day, I surprised her by volunteering to do the translation. With some hesitation, Mamita and El investigador agreed. At least from then on, our private matters did not have to be shared with our neighbors. My siblings soon caught up with their language skills, and we all became translators for our parents whenever El investigador visited, or when we went shopping, or when we had to go to the apartment project's management office. We all experienced the humiliation of El investigador's intrusive questions, but we were proud to be of help to our parents.

Our parents were suspicious and afraid of the very different and dangerous world that we lived in. They were determined that we would not be influenced by street-smart kids who experienced crime, drugs and alcohol and who inescapably ended up as dropouts, in jail or casualties. Our parents lived in fear that we would become statistics, so they were very strict and kept us rather secluded from the outside world. We were not allowed to socialize with our peers—no sleepovers, no visits. The girls were supervised 24/7, but the boys had a little more freedom. They were allowed to go to the park or to the neighborhood pool, but always with a time limit. We were all church goers and participated in the various church groups. Wally and Radames were altar boys; Elba, Miriam and I were members of the 'Daughters of Mary.' The Monteros were known in the parish as an exemplary family. Nonetheless, I hated to go to the required monthly confession because, try as I might to mask my voice, the priest would always recognize me. We all cringed during the 'fire and brimstone' sermons that the Jesuit priest delivered on Good Fridays.

Our outings were all family events. Mamá, Tía Carmen and her family had moved an hour away to The Bronx, so we often took the subway to their home where we spent the day playing with our four cousins. In the summer we rode the subway to Coney Island for a day at the beach and the amusement park. We loved to hang onto Papito while we tried to swim in the ocean. In the afternoon we would ride the Carousel and reach for the gold ring for a free ride. We always ended the day at Nathan's for their famous fried shrimp with tartar sauce. (Mom never touched that strange white American sauce.) Family events like birthdays, Christmas and New Years were always dancing opportunities. We learned how to dance all the Spanish dances—from the traditional Danza and Plena to the Guaracha, Cha Cha and

Mambo which was transitioning into the modern Salsa.

Summers must have been tough for Mom to keep her growing brood under control. We didn't go to summer or day camps offered by the neighborhood Settlement Houses because that was part of 'the world we had to be protected from.' So we spent a lot of time at home. The boys pushed for more play time in the park and got it, while Mom would accompany the girls to the playground. She would sit on a bench talking with the other Hispanic mothers and taking in the sun. But Mom had to get back to the house to clean, wash and cook, and that meant that we spent a lot of our apartment time engaged in our favorite pastime, reading. We were allowed to go to the local library by ourselves, and even though it was only three blocks away, it was a big deal to be allowed to go alone. The dangers, though, were not Mom's imagination—Pop had been robbed at knife point in our own elevator. Once on our way to the library, we came across a man in an open raincoat, revealing too much, and from then on we took another route.

We are all bookworms and always were. In the summers, we withdrew the maximum allotment of books and read them all within the six weeks' allotment of time to keep them. The stories in those books took us to places we couldn't even dream of visiting: fairy tales, adventure stories like Robinson Crusoe and Journey to the Center of the Earth, the entire Louisa May Alcott collection and more. I worked my eyes so much one summer that I needed glasses when I started school in September. Then by December, because I actually read less during school, I no longer needed the glasses. All that reading did wonders for my reading scores!

We lived our lives on two cultural tracks—the Puerto Rican home and the American school. At home we were a traditional Puerto Rican family. We ate Puerto Rican food: rice and beans, tomato sauces seasoned with golden home-made *sofrito*, chicken browned in a skillet, salted cod fish, plantain, green bananas and root vegetables like yuca, ñame and yautía. Then at school in Home Economics, we were taught that the healthy American diet was steak, potatoes and green vegetables, while our school friends talked about hamburgers and hotdogs. One day, Radamés complained to Mom that she should be making steak and potatoes, with green vegetables like the *Americanos*. Mom was furious because she worked hard to serve us healthy, freshly made meals, better than when she was a little girl. She also saw the complaint as a challenge to our ethnicity. As an adult, Radamés remembers this episode and realizes how ironic it was that later revisions of 'the healthy diet' proved Mom so right. We actually did eat a very healthy diet. Today, we consider it a treat to eat Mom's home-made Puerto Rican meals.

Within two years, we were all speaking English. As we became fluent in English, the five of us began to speak to each other in English. This upset Mom because she didn't understand us. Pop learned enough English to carry on a conversation and get the gist of our fast-paced discussions in English. His interaction with people at work, store owners, subway attendants, etc, all helped him learn English. Mom, on the other hand, stayed home with her kids, plus she had us to translate for her. Mamita became 'Mita' when addressing her and 'Mom' when talking among ourselves; Papito became 'Pop.' I changed the spelling of my name from Silvia to Sylvia, as another way to fit into the culture around me. Our Three Kings Day gave way to Christmas. With time, the star filled skies of Puerto Rico, the tropical showers and the freedom of playing all day out in the sun or 'under the house' all receded into happy childhood memories 'before the move.' Mom and Pop spoke about going 'home' some day.

Christmas must have continued to be a big challenge for Mom and Pop. They tried very hard to save us from envying other kids' toys. A couple of Christmases, they actually struck a deal with us. One year we wanted bicycles but we could only afford a single one. So we agreed that the bicycle would be a communal Christmas gift that we would share; we got a lot of pleasure from that one bike. To teach us to ride the bike, Pop and Mom would take us to the East River Park and Pop would run alongside, letting go without our realizing it. We loved it! Another year I really, really wanted a typewriter. Since I had learned to type in Junior High School, in High School I wanted to turn in typewritten papers. Once again we agreed on a communal gift and we got our money's worth, so much so that Miriam took the same machine to college with her.

In Junior High School I was given the choice to study a foreign language. Without hesitation I chose Spanish. Other kids thought I was just looking for an easy 'A,' but it wasn't that at all.

When I came to Nueva York, I was already reading and writing Spanish. I could read Pop's Spanish newspaper. I used my Spanish all the time when I interpreted for my parents. But as English became my dominant language, I was starting to grasp for words in Spanish. There was also the permeation of 'Spanglish' in our neighborhood. I wanted to be as fluent and accurate in Spanish as I was in English. Sometimes when I didn't know the correct word in Spanish, I felt I was losing something important to my identity. So even at that early age, there was a statement about pride in my roots. The kids were right about how easy Spanish was the first couple of years. Mom and Pop spoke very good Spanish and I had the two years of school in Puerto Rico. When I forgot a rule, I would speak the sentence in my head and the right answer would be there. But I did clean up some misspellings and I started culling Spanglish from my vocabulary. I continued studying Spanish through High School, where third- and fourth-year Spanish became much more challenging: complicated conjugations, sentence structures, reading comprehension, with analysis of Spanish poetry, short stories and novels.

The Lower East Side of the 1960's and 1970's was a somewhat mixed neighborhood. Once a center of Jewish culture, it still had a sizeable Jewish population. The mostly blue-collar Hispanic population was growing fast along with the beginnings of an overflow from Chinatown and Little Italy. The Williamsburg Bridge connected Manhattan and Brooklyn along Delancey Street. South of the Williamsburg Bridge, the Grand Street area was predominantly Jewish; north of the bridge it was predominantly Hispanic. The stores were owned by Jewish merchants who usually learned Spanish for their largely Spanish-speaking clientele. Sometimes I wasn't sure if a word was English or Yiddish—tumult, crotchety, chutzpa. The public schools were also similarly populated. In those days, the kids were assigned to advanced or regular classes according to their academic achievement. The Monteros soon worked our way to the more advanced classes that were mostly filled with Jewish kids.

Sara was my best friend in grammar school, a very bright, fun-loving Jewish girl. She and I were inseparable in school, although we never visited each other's homes. We were best friends and we enjoyed competing academically. In sixth grade, we competed for an accelerated Junior High School program—two years instead of three. Only one of us would be selected, and I was very hopeful that it would be me. The accelerated program would make up for the year I lost when I arrived in New York—I would no longer be older than the other kids in class. That wasn't to be, though, because Sara was selected. And so I lost my best friend to another school, and we lost contact until we met up again in High School. The teachers explained that they felt I would benefit more from the full three years having so recently arrived (four years before) from Puerto Rico. I went on to the local Junior High School where I graduated Valedictorian.

As much as we didn't appreciate our strict upbringing, there must have been something to it. We had a strong nuclear family, and we had no doubt that we were loved. The discipline at home made it a good place to study, and Mom was formidable in her expectations of us. Yet, she was surprisingly tolerant when we experienced difficulty in school. When she felt bad that she couldn't help, she encouraged the older ones to help the others. She didn't demand A's although we brought home many. B's were just as good as A's. To the occasional C or rare D, she would tell us to do the best we could. What she did demand was good behavior, and that was the first thing she looked for in our report cards. We were all good students. Wally went to Aviation High School in Long Island; Rod went to the prestigious Stuyvesant High School; Elba went to the High School of Art and Design; and Miriam set new records with a scholarship to a private middle school in the Village followed by another scholarship to the exclusive United Nations International School. I went to the neighborhood academic High School, Seward Park HS, where I was assigned to the honors program.

My sole focus in school was on getting the grades needed for a scholarship to college. I loved school and I studied for A's. Anything less was a major disappointment—agony. Sadly, other kids perceived this attitude toward academic achievement, along with our social distance, as arrogance. There were some frightening experiences in grammar school and Junior High School, when I became the target of the school bullies. In grammar school, my uncle Julio once again came to the rescue by having a good conversation with the school principal, which took care of the problem. In Junior High School, bullies waited for me after school intent on beating me up. Luckily, my two brothers were there to defend me. The bullies were always the kids with the worst grades and behavior problems.

The honors program in high school was extraordinary. Seward Park had the advantage of the most advanced, sometimes experimental, programs. The demographics of the student population reflected the

35

local neighborhood—mostly Hispanic and Jewish kids with a smattering of Italian, Chinese and African-American. The honors classes were mostly filled with Jewish kids and one or two minorities. The Jewish kids were economically better off; they dressed better; they had educated parents speaking English at home, so their conversational English was excellent and they were confident. The most stress I experienced was in English classes, where I felt I was at a distinct disadvantage. In those honors classes, we covered the most advanced works of literature and then discussed them in class. In creative writing, to my horror, we had to write our own short story. I was paralyzed by the fear of making a fool of myself and kept procrastinating. Finally, I decided to write about something I knew and that had affected me deeply, Mamá's death a couple of years earlier. Written in the first person in the voice of a young girl losing her grandmother, the story's vocabulary didn't have to be very advanced. What pride when I saw the A+++ on the three-page story and the professor asked me to read it out loud. Whew, I began to realize that the fear was inside me and that maybe I could control it.

In High School, I qualified for a special work program that placed me in the Attendance Office during my free period and introduced me to my first true mentor, Mr. Steinfeld. He took a lot of interest in me; he asked questions; he listened; he looked at my notes; and he comforted me when I didn't get my mandatory 'A.' He trusted me. Delightfully, my grammar school best friend Sara also went to Seward Park High School. Because she had gone through the accelerated Junior High School program, she was one year ahead of me, yet she was no longer in the honors program. In fact, she was way back with the problem kids. One day, not too long after I had started working in the Attendance Office, she came to see me. My happiness at seeing her lasted until she asked me to look through private student records for the home address and phone of a boy she liked. I refused and, with the lost of trust, we never spoke again. I was very upset that my grammar school friend only came to see me to take advantage of my position in the Attendance Office. And I thought back on the decision that my teachers had made selecting her for the special program over me. I would never have squandered that opportunity.

One day, Mr. Steinfeld asked me to tutor his nephew Joseph, who was struggling with ninth-grade Algebra. With my parents' permission, I walked to Joseph's home in the Grand Street area three times a week for $3.00 an hour. Nine dollars a week was a lot of money and came in very handy for some of my school expenses. To everyone's delight, Joseph's grades in Algebra improved. That was my first teaching success, and it reinforced my growing desire to become a teacher.

The day finally arrived when our parents voluntarily dropped out of the Welfare program. Mom was making a little extra money baby-sitting, we were all teenagers and took advantage of work/study opportunities and Wally was off to the Air Force. The surprised social worker insisted that we still qualified for Welfare but enough was enough. It was a big step—freedom from the price we paid for charity.

Precisely because of my family's welfare experience, it is an honor to be in a position to help other people. One of the important lessons learned is to help others in a way that is both helpful and not demeaning. As a related story, the mother of the young man I was tutoring knew that my family and I were going to Puerto Rico for the first time since our arrival. On the last day of tutoring, she gave me a gift bag, almost a full wardrobe of clothing—tights, slacks, blouses—an incredibly nice thing to do. Yet I walked out of the house embarrassed to be receiving charity again. If the gift had consisted of one item, great, but a suitcase full of clothing was too much of a different message. Had I been so poorly dressed every time I visited her home? How could I ever explain that to her? I didn't even try. But while I never faulted her for my feelings, it became clear that sometimes a showering of gifts is not the wisest gift.

This was the year when all our savings went toward the long awaited trip 'home.' Nine years after arriving in Nueva York in 1966, we went back to Puerto Rico; I was sixteen years old. Pop stayed for a week because he had to come back to work but we stayed for three weeks. We stayed at Abuelo and Abuela's house – the same little wooden house they lived in when we left for Nueva York. The rock in front of their house was smaller than we remembered and the trail to our old house seemed narrower. Our little house was still standing but no longer in use. The mosquitoes were ferocious and left large welts on our no longer sun-cured skin. We had trouble with the heavy humidity and heat, and the bugs were frightening, but the stars were just as numerous and bright; the sky bluer than blue and running in the rain was still a treat. We reconnected with family and friends and then returned to our other 'home.'

In my senior year, Mr. Steinfeld encouraged me to apply to Barnard College of Columbia University. My goals had been more modest— City University—but I took my mentor's advice and applied. I was surprised to get a call for an interview and more so when I was accepted with a full scholarship.

I graduated Salutatorian from High School which required that I give the welcoming speech on graduation day. Once again I agonized over the speech and the fact that I would be speaking in front of hundreds of people. A school friend was so proud that a Puerto Rican was getting this honor that one day he said to me, "You are the pride of Puerto Rico." I thought about this as I worked on my speech. What would be my message? Then I saw the reverse should be true—that I should be the one proud, proud of who I am and of my Puerto Rican heritage. So I had my message, and I went a step further and wrote half my speech in Spanish so the Hispanics in the audience who didn't speak English well—my parents included—would be able to understand me. I observed the uncomfortable shifting in seats by the non-Spanish speakers as I explained this to the audience and went on in Spanish to a spontaneous applause by the Spanish-speaking audience. And so off to a different and frightening Ivy League world.

Marriage
and College

My future husband migrated from Puerto Rico to live at my aunt's apartment in the Bronx. He had dropped out of high school and came to New York to make a living. He was one of the few non-family young men that I interacted with on a regular basis. We were not allowed to date, but because he lived at my aunt's place, we saw each other often. So, even as I worked through the academic and social challenges of high school, my parallel cultural life was moving along a more predictable course—during my senior year in high school, I was engaged to be married.

Our courtship was very traditional: He formally asked my parents for my hand in marriage and came courting on agreed days. Although my parents were dismayed that I would be married so young, 19 wasn't an unusual age for Hispanic girls. Mom had married at 17. I would be married at 19. Not surprisingly, they did express their expectation that I 'be allowed' to continue my education, and my fiancé agreed. Still, my own dismay was silent: from my perspective, no one but I had a voice in that decision, even if I were married.

We didn't go out alone until immediately before we got married, when we went to look at the apartment we were renting. During this year of courtship, I was in my senior year of high school – still very focused on my studies. The fact that my fiancé had dropped out of school bothered me but he assured me that he would finish High School. I pictured us working and studying together, excited by the thought of my own place, doing my own thing and making my own decisions. We were married during my freshman year at Barnard. He worked in a distribution center while I focused on the requirements of a full time student and the rhythm method of birth control endorsed by the Catholic Church. A year later, my beautiful little boy, Kenneth, was born.

I knew early in our marriage that it wasn't going well. My husband's wages were minimal, poverty is not as romantic as it sounds and I wasn't happy. Our tenement apartment in the Lower East Side was similar to the first apartment I had lived in when we first arrived in New York. Once again, the cockroaches. Worse, the bathtub was in the kitchen with our toilet (in the hallway) shared with the next-door neighbor. The boiler often broke down, and the owners took their time repairing it. The building was also a haven for drug dealers. I became active in a government-sponsored program focused on clearing the community of crime and drugs. When the drug dealers figured this out, they in turn put the pressure on us to get out. One evening, we came home to a vandalized apartment. Thieves had actually broken through the wall above the security gate that protected the doorway. We could see their footprints—on the ceiling. We lost our small stereo and what little jewelry there was.

But the most traumatic experience came late one cold night. Kenny's crying awakened me to what seemed like a fog inside the bedroom. The acrid smell down my throat sent a cold shiver through me. I was instantly alert, in a state of panic, realizing we were in a smoke-filled room, screaming, "Oh my God, the apartment's on fire!" I grabbed screaming Kenny and bolted for the door, only to be met with a thicker wall of smoke. The fire had been set in the exterior hallway against an unused door that led straight into my bedroom—exactly where we had placed the crib. I quickly closed the door and ran with the baby to the living room where the smoke hadn't reached and where I could get out through the fire escape, if necessary. I was terrified to climb down six flights of a rickety fire escape in thirty-degree weather carrying a struggling baby. With trembling fingers, I dialed 911, and the operator said stay inside because the firemen would be there in minutes. Kenny had quieted down and was settled on the sofa. While I waited for the firemen to arrive, I threw a bucket of water at the flames in the hallway.

The whole event was literally a scary wake-up call. We moved to another building as quickly as we could. I also immediately began to petition the Housing Authority for an apartment. It took a couple of years, but we were finally granted an apartment in the projects.

Meanwhile, I continued to carry a full course load at Barnard College. My time there was an extraordinary life-changing experience. Thanks to Mr. Steinfeld for steering me in the direction of Barnard College and to Barnard for the financial aid that made it possible. Barnard was my introduction to a world beyond my dreams—a world filled with very confident women. It was a no-nonsense learning environment where I interacted and competed with some of the brightest young women in the country. The quality of education was one that only the mention of Ivy League or Seven Sisters can evoke. (Barnard College shares the distinction of The Seven Sisters along with Bryn Mawr, Mount Holyoke, Radcliffe, Smith, Vassar and Wellesley.) Here I was in this environment during the turmoil of the late 1960's, marveling at how freely my classmates challenged the establishment, our government and other governments around the world. Some of the most memorable debates occurred spontaneously between classes in the study halls. These spur-of-the-moment gatherings where we exercised the right to tackle any national or international issue taught me to have an opinion about what was going on in the outside world. Yet when Barnard women joined the Ivy League men across Broadway—Columbia University—in a sit-down to protest our involvement in Vietnam, it was not in me to join them. Instead I walked through the demonstrators and went to class, but not because I supported the war. Not at all. I wanted my brother back. But because I couldn't snub the amazing college that handed me the gift of this magnificent education. Between the church and my home, my world had been one of do's and don'ts, rules and regulations, 'shoulds' that I mostly obeyed. I was there to study and get my degree.

When I was pregnant during the first semester of my sophomore year, the subway ride from the Lower East Side up to Barnard at 116th Street was especially nauseating. The waitress at the small campus café would give me a spoonful of cola extract to settle my stomach before class. The baby arrived late in February, it was a difficult labor, and I was unable to return to school that semester. The professors assured my friends at school that I would not return for the typical scenario: young Hispanic, married and starting to have children. If the statistics played out, chances were that indeed there would be no return. And in fact, I came close to making just that decision.

That spring and summer, I worked at the same company as my husband. I had worked there a couple of summers and had moved up to the front office, solving the mysteries of incorrect or incomplete shipments. I enjoyed that detective work, and the office personnel gave me encouraging praise. As September approached—time to go back to school—I was offered a full-time job. That was the only time in my life that seriously tempted me to drop out of college. I was living in a ghetto apartment and now I had a baby. My husband's salary was barely enough to pay the rent and our growing needs. Mom was taking care of the baby for whatever I could give her, sometimes nothing. And so when I was offered a chance to make a whopping $125 a week, it was a serious temptation. It would take so much pressure out of our lives. I considered the offer for about a week and getting very, very depressed. I thought about my lifelong goal, about the professors who knowingly assured my friends that I would not return and my friends responding, "But you don't know Sylvia!"

To my professors' shock and my friends' delight, September saw me back at school, determined to make up the lost semester and graduate with my class. I studied every summer after that and packed twenty credits into normal semesters. My parents kept Kenny overnight on the nights before exams or when a paper was due, to allow me to work into the night. Despite a full scholarship at Barnard, though, books and commuting expenses were not covered. A small student loan every year paid for the books and supplies. A part-time job helped with clothing, lunch and travel money.

Socializing during college because of my responsibilities to my husband, my son, my household and part-time job was completely out. Taking the earliest classes in the morning meant that 3:00 p.m. clocked me on my way to work. After work—over to Mom's to pick up Kenny and then home to make dinner and study. But I did have a circle of friends. The Spanish Studies department was small enough that I had the same group of women in my literature classes. My best friend from High School also made it to Barnard and roomed at the dorms. Her growing circle of friends became my circle as well. During my junior year, my sister Miriam earned her own scholarship to Barnard and she, too, roomed at the dorms. However, there weren't many other women at Barnard who were dealing with the issues I was dealing with. Money, husband, baby, cultural expectations.

I graduated together with my class, a major in Spanish Studies and a minor in Education, and went straight to Graduate School at Queens College. The decision to attend Queens for my Masters was easy. Attending some ASPIRA events, an organization for developing educational and leadership capacity in Hispanic youth, I met a professor from the Spanish department at Queens. He saw to it that I was offered a part-time teaching position at the undergraduate level if I went to Queens for my Masters. No decision there.

When my husband and my parents realized my studies would continue beyond the undergraduate, they were somewhat surprised. A teaching job in the New York City Board of Education was only a license away, with all the requirements under my belt. Shouldn't I get the job and start making money? But the decision to stay in college after my son was born meant going as far as I could. A PhD was within my sights and very valuable in the teaching field. Although I had planned to start teaching in high schools, my goal then shifted towards teaching at the university level. So off I went to graduate school.

Meanwhile, my marriage was in serious trouble. My husband never went back to school, and we were growing farther and farther apart. He could not share my agony of studying for finals or writing four term papers a semester. He couldn't share the joy of a good grade average. We lived in different social worlds; we couldn't bring our circles of friends together. Neither could we reconcile our own significant personal differences.

The money that I earned teaching at the undergraduate level paid for my Master's Degree and allowed me to get my teaching license in New York City public high schools. During this period, my parents were still very much in the picture with Mom continuing to babysit

Kenny. Memories are very vivid of the bus ride between my apartment and my parents', carrying my son on one arm and my schoolbag strapped over the other shoulder. Once a week, Mom would do the laundry I brought over while I sat in class. Often she would make dinner for us as well. Today I marvel not only at Mom's unwavering support but also at the seemingly endless source of energy that allowed me to do all that.

Then the unthinkable happened. My final Masters Degree requirements consisted of an essay exam and an oral exam. I did well on the written exam but as the day of the orals approached got very nervous. By the time I walked into the room, I was terrified. I faced a panel of four professors, white men, who could question me about anything in Spanish literary history. The fears that I had struggled so hard to conquer as a little girl came back to me like a tsunami. And I froze to the point where I couldn't get a sound out of my throat. I knew that I had failed and still couldn't believe it. After the exam, I sought out my program sponsor. Embarrassed that I let him down, all I could think to ask was when I could take the exam again. Six months. I went home crying. But for the next six long months, my focus was on preparing to retake the exam; I studied with friends, spent hours at the library, read and summarized and outlined. I reviewed everything I had studied related to Spanish studies—history, literature, architecture, etc. Six months later, I presented for the orals again. One tranquilizer and I aced the exam.

While studying and cramming to retake the orals at Queens College, I received my first teaching assignment from the New York City Board of Education at Jane Addams Vocational High School, an all girls' school. Finally, a full-time job. As a teacher, I couldn't wait to meet my students. But I was in for a rude awakening. In that year of 1974, the City and the Teachers' Association did not agree on the terms of a new contract, and the school year began with a teacher strike. This time I couldn't walk through the picket line: I had no choice but to spend my first two days 'on the job' walking a picket line instead. The powers that be resolved their differences very quickly after that, but the teachers were fined for two days on the picket line. What a way to start my dream career.

The South Bronx had a large low-income Hispanic population, and Jane Addams Vocational High School reflected those demographics. Many of the girls were recent immigrants from the Caribbean, learning English as their second language. Their situations brought back vivid memories of my own experience, and I could just feel what they were going through. Most of the girls were there to study cosmetology, and their interest in academic subjects was limited. It was exhausting work for me, but I was rewarded by the few who got it. I could tell who had strong family disciplines, who were dealing with self-esteem issues, who wasn't interested in school at all—too much in a rush to get to work and make some money. The audacity of some of the girls, merciless in the creative ways they came up with to keep their handsome male teachers off balance, quite shocked me. One of those men was thrown off balance, red-faced, deer in the headlights, when one of the girls took off her blouse in the middle of his class. But, in spite of the surprises that only teenagers can come up with, Jane Addams was a good learning environment, fortunate to have a teaching staff that cared and a fabulous department head who took her work seriously. Her feedback helped refine my teaching skills.

But I still lived in the projects! I was making $8,500 a year as a teacher. Although we had a little more breathing room, we still could not afford to move out of subsidized housing. I was able to buy a used car to make my commute much easier, but with tires so threadbare, I had to learn how to change my own tires. One morning I was terrified to find that all four tires had been slashed. Our housing apartment was burglarized, and for the second time I lost what little jewelry I had accumulated. This time, I almost walked in on the burglars. Is this all that my life was going to be? God, couldn't it get a little easier?

Our marriage was no better, but I was committed to doing all I could to make it work; marriage in the Catholic Church meant no divorce. I sought marriage counseling through Catholic Charities, where we were assigned a wonderful nun as our counselor. After two years, even our nun admitted it: our incompatibility was insurmountable.

The decision to get a divorce was mine, one I had to make on my own and the toughest I've ever made. It meant disrupting my son's life and redefining the relationship with my church, indeed with the family. Even though my parents and siblings were very supportive, my parents were quite let down. Breaking the sacrament of marriage is so serious in the Catholic Church that the only way out is to agree that the marriage was null and void to begin with. I wasn't happy to declare that, especially since Kenny came from that marriage.

The emotional recovery took years while I worked through it internally, dipping once more into my own source of strength and optimism. Yet, I wouldn't change a thing. The experience of marriage and divorce accelerated my development as an individual, as a human being and as a mother. I am who I am today because of these experiences. With the perspective only time and maturity can bring, I came to accept equal responsibility for our failed marriage. We were two good people looking for happiness in two very different and irreconcilable worlds. As a family of two, my son and I developed a very special bond.

The year 1976 crammed multiple hard to face challenges in it. While I was devastated when I failed my Master's Degree orals, I was ecstatic when I sailed through them six months later; I filed and got my divorce; then, unexpectedly, I also got my pink slip from the Board of Education. A graduate degree, single again and jobless. That summer, my parents fulfilled their dream to return to Puerto Rico where they bought their first home. I stayed in New York hoping that the city school system would reassign me. Despite some substitute teaching, it was clear that a reassignment wasn't going to happen quickly. Kenny was also missing his grandparents terribly. Having taken care of him since birth, they were his second set of parents. After the disruption of his parents' divorce and two moves, separation from his grandparents was beyond him. Penniless, lonely and needing to do something, I sought my parents. Within days, I got two airline tickets in the mail and I too went 'home' to Puerto Rico.

My teaching experiences at Queens College and New York City High Schools would get me in the door at the local University. Even more than on the mainland, a Masters' Degree would further my career in Puerto Rico. Prior to the trip, I had submitted my resume to Inter-American University, and it paid off: within a week of arriving in Puerto Rico, I walked into the classroom to teach. This was an exciting day because teaching at the university level was a long-term goal, but here I was, 26 years old. A chain of distressing events had led to another dream come true.

Career Change

After 19 years, I was home, and I wasn't homesick for New York. I delighted in the deep blue skies, the hot sun and warm ocean water. Lush, tropical trees and flowering plants created a perpetual spring. Tropical showers were torrential but brief, and the hot sun would dry everything within minutes. I tried to recapture what over the years had become lyrical childhood memories, pointing out every detail to Kenny with the hope that he wouldn't take any of it for granted.

Kenny started first grade at the local grammar school, and my parents continued to care for him as they had done in New York. My amazing parents had also bought me a car. Knowing that in Puerto Rico it was an absolute necessity, they spent what little they had left after buying the house. Thankfully, because I started working so quickly, I was able to help out with expenses.

At Inter-American University, I taught Spanish literature and language for non-native speakers. To my surprise, there was a significant population of non-Spanish-speaking Americans in the area, most of whom were expatriates from the mainland. One of my students worked at Arnar-Stone Laboratories, a small pharmaceutical company located nearby. One day she asked if I would be interested in doing some translations for the company. They were required to provide policies and procedures in Spanish for their non-English-speaking employees. This actually sounded very interesting to me, plus I could make some money on the side. And so, for the next six months, my evenings were filled with lesson plans and with translations. The translations were more challenging than I had anticipated, because the content was technical, and although I used a technical dictionary, I needed to interview the local staff to fully understand what I was translating. In this way, I met all of the leaders and many production employees. I was impressed with their work and looked forward to the visits: Arnar-Stone made only one product—a medicine to be injected in the heart when a patient was in cardiac arrest—truly a life saving drug. I also translated personnel policies. This was my introduction to the field of Personnel and I was fascinated.

The second semester at Inter-American University I picked up a third course. As a result, I was preparing three distinctly different lesson plans. In the meantime, Arnar-Stone began recruiting for the top personnel position at the site, and the local management team wanted me for the job. What a dilemma. Inter-American University had me off to a good start, yet I was fascinated by this new field of Personnel. I decided to apply for the job and tackle the dilemma *mañana*. Arnar-Stone's Vice President of Human Resources flew into Puerto Rico for the interview.

Granted that I didn't know anything about Personnel except what I learned translating the Personnel Policies. In fact, I knew more about the manufacturing process than about the Personnel function. But since local management wanted me for the position, they patiently prepared me for the interview, drilling me on the acronyms they thought I should know. What is OSHA? Occupational Safety and Health Administration. What is *Fondo del Seguro del Estado?* Puerto Rico's Workmen's

Compensation. What is the EEOC? Equal Employment Opportunity Commission. Dr. Cane, the site Director who would be my boss, also reviewed the corporate structure with me. Local Arnar-Stone managers were on a mission, really quite humorous. And so I crammed for the interview and presented myself feeling optimistic, energized and ready to take on the world as only a 27 year old can.

When Arnar-Stone offered me the position, the University countered with a full-time professorship. *Mañana* had arrived. Time to tackle that dilemma. The University offer was a dream come true, and my parents were appalled that I would even consider not accepting it. A position at the University was much more secure than in industry. Yet the field of Personnel was new and exciting. The management team was very likable. And the salary difference was significant, with Arnar-Stone's offer 50% higher than the University's offer. But I didn't want my decision to be based either on money, exclusively, or on playing it safe.

It is still amazing how effortless the career change was, in part because there was little to lose as far as a standard of living: I didn't owe money or own much of anything. My positive attitude was ever-present. Things would work out. Why look back?

My experience at Arnar-Stone equated to an undergraduate degree in Human Resources. The Vice President of Human Resources had given me a book entitled *Personnel Management* that served as a beginner's course in college like Personnel 101. Another marvelous mentor, Dr. Cane, taught me how a biochemist could make his career in the pharmaceutical industry. He steered me in directions that would accelerate my knowledge of Human Resources, encouraging me to join the Pharmaceutical Personnel Association, where I met my counterparts in over thirty similar companies in Puerto Rico. What an eye-opening experience, to learn about local labor laws, compensation and benefits. Dr. Cane also had tremendous patience even for the most basic questions. He coached me through the politics of the headquarters office and the benefits of networking with the experts in Illinois. I was encouraged and steered not just by Dr. Cane, but by the other leaders in the company as well, and my trips to Illinois headquarters were positive learning experiences.

I was working hard and loving every minute of it. For the first time, my income was enough to cover my needs which included helping my parents with household expenses. I moved Kenny to the private parochial school in town where he would get a better education. At the same time, I was experiencing the biggest gift that Puerto Rico could give me—I was no longer a minority. All but two of my colleagues were Puerto Rican, and the two American expatriates demonstrated tremendous enthusiasm and respect for the culture—my culture. My formerly defensive pride blossomed into genuine appreciation for my roots, my history, and the breathtaking island of Puerto Rico.

As my first anniversary with Arnar-Stone approached, the Vice President of Human Resources probed my interest in moving to the corporate offices in Illinois. This was very flattering, but I wasn't ready for another major move so soon. Kenny was doing well in school, so I didn't want to put him through the trauma either. In addition, it would be harder to be a single parent in Illinois where I didn't know anyone.

Locally, Dr. Cane asked whether I would be interested in a production position. My translation work had taught me so much about the production process that I was able to serve as tour guide when senior leaders visited from Illinois. I briefly considered whether I wanted another major career change. Arnar-Stone Puerto Rico was a very small site with only 65 employees. Soon I would need a bigger challenge. I decided to continue in the Personnel field but knew that to grow professionally in Puerto Rico, I would have to look at other companies.

Before long, Pfizer, Puerto Rico approached me. The Personnel

Manager, who I had met in the Personnel Association, asked me about a position in his own group. Eighteen months after joining Arnar-Stone and eternally grateful, I handed in my resignation with a heavy heart; a remarkable company that took a chance on me, with wonderful managers who took me under their wings, helped me make a successful career transition and reinforced my belief in myself.

I joined Pfizer at the age of 29 and for the first time I experienced how dramatically different company cultures can be. As open and flexible an environment as Arnar-Stone was, so Pfizer had more structured Human Resources systems and the heavier presence of Divisional and Corporate Headquarters of a considerably larger organization. It would take me longer to reach the comfort level I enjoyed and really missed at my old company. Miserable at first, I refused to leave, give up and admit failure. First I had to be successful, then I could go to another company. The transition took six months until I was doing so well, I wouldn't even think of leaving—a wonderful lesson about transitions, company cultures and patience. Without anticipating I would spend the rest of my career with Pfizer, stay I did. As Pfizer prospered, I thrived. A 28 ½-year career brought me back to New York, took me around the world multiple times, taught me most of the company's businesses and supplied numerous life-long friendships. I surpassed many dreams, previously undefined.

Here my linear story ends. Having given voice to the story of my experiences, I will now allow the voice of experience to interpret the rest of the story. My introspective themes cut across a long career. After twenty-eight and a half years, I retired from Pfizer's highest Human Resources position and Pfizer had become the largest pharmaceutical company in the world.

No plumbing or electricity, the little house on stilts was located in the middle of the plantation where our father worked. This sketch was drawn from an old photo taken fifteen years later, not long before the house was demolished.

We treasure this irreplaceable family photo. We walked three miles each way to the photographer in town. Front row, left to right: Radames (age 7), Sylvia (5), Miriam (2), Elba (3). Top row, left to right: Eligia (26), Cruz (32), Waldemar (8).

New York was a shock. We missed playing outdoors. This photo was taken the day we arrived from Puerto Rico. Left to right: Radames (8), Elba (6) Sylvia (7).

Total immersion in English helped Sylvia speak English very quickly. By third grade (age 9), she was bilingual. Back row, 4th from right.

For Cruz and Eligia's 45th anniversary, we posed to replicate our young family photo. The girls had to sit, and Radames stood beside Mom. Front row: Sylvia, Miriam, Elba; Top row: Radames, Eligia, Cruz, Waldemar.

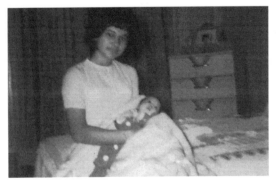

Sylvia was a young mother at age 20.

Sylvia and son, Kenny, simultaneously thought "Thank God" at his college graduation.

Baby talk turned Abuela Sylvia into 'Bella.' The best things in life are grandchildren—Kenny Jr. and Miranda.

Global integrations called for frequent travel in cars, planes, trains and helicopters.

Strategic meetings with leaders from around the world were frequent and necessary for global alignment. Sylvia wore bright red in a sea of navy and gray.

Long flights brought quiet time to catch up on work.

As responsibilities grew, the ability to address large groups became a critical skill for success. Yet it took Sylvia many years to conquer the fear of public speaking.

"I thought about the road that led me to the boardroom, and I could not contain a smile of pride as I remembered the beginning ..."

After 32 years as a bachelorette and 18 years of courting, Sylvia married her best friend, O.B.

Part Three
Self-Confidence

Value Who
You Are and
What You Are

*Others do not define you or who you are. You are more powerful
than their notions of you. You are free to achieve and excel.*

A little seven-year-old newly arrived in New York from Puerto
Rico, I quickly learned we were inferior. Suddenly we became the
subject of mistreatment sometimes oppressive. The words 'immigrant'
and 'minority' forced their way into our vocabulary. This was a new
experience for us. Born American citizens, we also took special pride in
being Puerto Rican Americans. Before long, we learned what it was like
to be called names, to hear slurs about our heritage. Soon I realized
there were barriers, major barriers, blocking my dreams.

The emotional memories of growing up in the Lower East Side of

Manhattan follow two streams. One stream thought me not as good as the *Americanos*. I didn't dress as well. I spoke English with an accent. We were on 'welfare' living in government subsidized housing. We had to submit to quarterly investigations from the Welfare Department, whose questions invaded our privacy and challenged our integrity. I picked up on the subtle and sometimes not so subtle messages from the people in power—they were in control, and their messages told me I was not as capable or as good.

But the other stream *knew* they were wrong. With a sense of anger, I knew I wasn't 'less than.' Less than what? I had the same potential as anybody else out there, maybe more. My strong family unit gave me love, solid values and deep faith. I was always a good student, one of the best in class. English came quickly, as did math, science, social studies. I aspired to be a teacher when I grew up. Along with my best friend in grammar school, a very bright Jewish girl, I got the best grades in class. Four years after arriving on the mainland, I could compete with the smartest girl in the class. This gave me the confidence that I could indeed be successful in this world.

However, for the longest time, the dominant stream was *I'm not as good as*. I internalized endless negative messages from classmates, teachers and other presumably wise adults, that I could not compete, that I could not succeed: the giggles when I mispronounced a word; the sideways glances at my home-sewn seams or scuffed shoes; the jokes about 'Spics' and our pointy shoes for killing cockroaches; the exclusion from mostly Caucasian social groups; the preferential treatment on the part of some teachers; the whispered comments from those same teachers when they thought I wasn't listening. These messages—some loud, some unsounded—insidiously threatened the core of my spirit. The result was to quiet me in class although I was a straight-A student. I was terrified of raising my hand and speaking up, of making mistakes, of showing others they were right—I wasn't as good as. When the teachers chose my best friend over me for a rare spot in an accelerated junior high school program, they reinforced this train of thought—I could not compete.

I came dangerously close to wishing I wasn't who I was. What would have happened to my sense of identity if I denied or were embarrassed to acknowledge who I was? There is no one else that I could claim to be. I would be a shadow, not even of myself, but of someone else.

On the other hand, there were angels whose behavior helped neutralize the negatives. My best friend in high school, again a very bright Jewish girl, showed genuine interest in listening to people and learning about their diversity. We were like scholastic twins in school— same classes, same focus on grades, same straight A's. Also, my mentor in high school encouraged me authentically, believed in me and told me so. Lastly was the prestige of being in the honors track throughout my high school years.

And there were our parents, who always expected their children to succeed. They made that very clear: they demanded it. Indeed, the entire dislocation from Puerto Rico was intended for our benefit. We never questioned their love. They impressed on us the value of an education beyond high school. But, if we were going to go to college, we would have to earn scholarships, and that meant we had to get excellent grades. I studied for A's, considered anything lower a failure, and even the infrequent B spelled agony.

One bad day in my senior year of high school, one of my own teachers was responsible for compiling a list of students who qualified for graduation class honors. He asked all students to raise hands if they had a four-year average equal to B+ or higher, and a number of us raised our hands. My average was up there, I was sure, but the teacher looked at me with disbelief. I was the only Hispanic in that honors class, and he came right out and asked me if I was sure.

In front of all the kids he asked, but why on earth did he ask me alone? I was humiliated. Bristling, but polite, I said, "Yes, I am." As it turned out, I had the second highest average in the graduating class and delivered the salutatorian speech both in English **and** in Spanish. I latched onto my ethnicity, improved my native Spanish and went out of my way to assert my roots.

The experience was a defining moment. Somewhere in the process of learning the rules of our society, the ins and outs of being a minority in America, I realized that discrimination was not my fault. I consciously decided not to allow someone else's problem (prejudice) to keep me from getting where I wanted to go. The lesson was a gift. It was a gift, because some people spend their entire lives wrestling with constant messages steeped in bias. It was a gift, and ever since then, for me, the whole dynamic of discriminatory behavior—whether in school, at work or in society—belonged to someone else—the discriminator. That was something I was not going to own. I was not going to wear that. Ever. That wonderful defining moment has stood me exceptionally well, with the opportunity to apply that belief many times as a professional.

No one could take away my belief in myself and pride in my roots. I knew what I was capable of. With hard work, I could achieve my goals in life. Yet other people tended to put me in a box. I had to figure out for myself how to crawl out of that limiting place, with its ridiculous assumptions. I didn't belong there, I saw no box, but I had to fight to get out. How do we, as young people just defining ourselves, really get to believe that others do not define us for who we are? That we're free from outside perceptions, more powerful than outside notions? Outer assumptions happen universally, with young people boxed in for different reasons. It might be the overweight girl or the short boy. Or it might be the African American or Asian girl, or the most recent immigrant. But it's the same box. There may have been no particular day or special event—but somewhere in the process of learning the rules of our society, it hit me that discrimination was the other person's problem and it wasn't going to limit me.

Why was discrimination the discriminator's problem? Because that is what kept the other person from knowing who I really was. The high school teacher whose question "Are you sure?" horrified me in class never knew who I was. Poor thing could not take pride in his own student. Even though I had been in his class all semester. Even though I carried the second highest average in the school. Discrimination—whether out of ignorance that is overt or subtle—created a disconnect between us. Once I was over my anger, my conclusion was that he was the one who had missed out on knowing who I truly was.

As a very personal reaction to discrimination, this type of thinking takes tremendous confidence and belief in oneself. Where did the confidence come from to deny others the power to make me feel bad about myself? No simple answer, but at the root are definitely my parents who kept drilling us, "You're smart, you're going to be better; you will do better than we were ever able to do. Education will give you choices." They demonstrated they could raise five kids in the middle of a drug-infested, high crime area of the city and remain separate from it. They fought hard to keep us from being 'contaminated' by the society they did not fully understand. They also modeled tremendous courage and strength that we in turn drew upon, moving five kids from Puerto Rico to a completely different society, culture and language. They struggled to fit in, to make a living, through humiliating experiences. It took formidable strength to do what they did, all so their children would be in a better place, a place of opportunities.

Amazingly, my parents were very humble people and also had pride in their work. Pop was the most humble man I've ever known. His

71

pride was in everything that he touched, and he did the best he could with great integrity. A janitor in a psychiatric hospital, he would come home some days beaming because the medical staff had complimented him on the spotlessness of his area. He would say, "My floors are the cleanest and shiniest in the hospital." He was very proud of that, never embarrassed to be a janitor. It was honest work, and he was the best janitor that he could be.

Mom was incredibly ambitious for us—it was all that mattered to her. Her determination was the force behind that risky move to New York. She dreaded that in Puerto Rico her kids were not going to be able to go to school much beyond where she did. The only way her kids were going to have more choices than their parents did was to improve the economic situation. Her ambition for her family was the quality that shaped us as we grew. My parents were two bright people trapped in poverty. But they had courage and ambition for their kids, a sense of pride and integrity that transferred solidly to us.

They gave us the extraordinary gift of self-esteem, an important factor for anybody. No matter what your circumstances, there probably are people close to you—parents, grandparents, mentors—who inspire you, who affirm and value who you are and give you the inner strength to succeed.

Our story follows a common American theme: 'We may not have had opportunities, but we want to make sure our children get them.' My siblings and I were fortunate to have a strong nuclear family, while many others are not as fortunate. Too many of our young people are growing up with the added challenge of an absent father, mother or both. What if you are in a really bad place, without the benefit of a strong family unit? The process has to be similar. That is, no matter what type of challenging situation you find yourself in, you must be able to dig in and find that strength inside as an individual. There's a pot of gold in there waiting for you to dig and find it.

The gold inside is the strength of will to overcome whatever hands you insurmountable odds. The gold is your belief in yourself and your freedom of action. "I am who I am. I matter. I am valuable. I have the ability to move positively forward from here. It's all my decision. I can decide to focus on my schoolwork. I can decide to turn down drugs; I can decide not to steal. Or I could decide I will do those things." Not to over simplify a complex situations, but in the end, it's largely your decision.

A former boss and mentor once crystallized this lesson, helping a work group become a better team. One of the team members complained that a colleague's behavior 'made him so angry.' My boss noted that in fact the team member had made a choice to become angry, suggesting "It's not like there's a chain connecting the two of you, allowing your colleague to pull the chain and trigger your reaction." That person does not control you, does not **make you** angry. **You** chose that specific response. You chose to be angry in reaction to what that person did or said. You could have chosen not to be angry; you could have chosen to laugh instead. You react and respond as a choice. But it is a choice.

It is when we think that we have no choice that we get into trouble. It's that strong, independent core inside you that will help you decide how your life will play out. Will you stay in school? You decide. Will you work hard for good grades? You decide. Will you seek out counselors to help you figure out how to go from high school to college? You decide. It's there for you to choose to do and to decide how to react when bad things happens.

Pick Yourself Up and Keep Going

Remember, the traumatic experience of failing the oral exam for my Masters Degree had little to do with subject matter knowledge and a lot to do with believing in myself. Facing that panel of professors paralyzed me with the old I-can't-compete fears. I could have given up, since I was already teaching and didn't need my Masters degree to continue teaching. But the thought of not completing my life-long goal was devastating. So, when I failed the first time, I didn't give up. Because the professors were faculty who knew the quality of my work, I could have blamed them, "They should have seen I was nervous and been a little more supportive." Instead, I picked myself up and kept going. I accepted full responsibility for my failure and, focusing on the future, immediately started to prepare myself to retake the exam at the earliest possible date. I turned my energy towards the goal, not the griping or remorse.

Too many people give up on their dreams when faced with very tough situations. Giving up follows them later in life, because they continue to see themselves in that lower echelon that has no right to aspire to the American dream. They deny themselves the dream, because they're trapped in that box created by others. But who would willingly step into that box?

In addressing diverse groups from high school students to professionals, I always make the point of valuing self and origin. This is where the most nods show, especially from minorities and women in the audience. They too have faced the challenge of negative messaging that they have come close to believing.

Regardless of your circumstances, you have the ability to choose, you don't have to believe those who tell you that you are somehow less than. First and foremost, value yourself and take pride in who you are. Unique. Special. A full human being. The feeling projects to others and is crucial to future success.

UPON REFLECTION,
here are some takeaways to
value who you are and what you are:

Self confidence comes from within. Never cede that power to others.

Crawl out of the limiting space and ridiculous assumptions
of being boxed in by others.

Only you choose how to react to bad things. Your reaction is not
automatic—it may be a habit, but it is still your choice.

Apply your energy towards the goal.
Don't waste time on griping or remorse.

Maintain a Positive and Proactive Attitude

These two attitudes reinforce each other.
Together they are an unstoppable combination.

Optimism may be an innate quality or one you develop, but it's not much more than looking at the bright side of things. No matter how deep a hole you are in, no matter how difficult the challenge, there is always a way out, a way to succeed. In a tough situation, use impatience as a motivator to do something—to act. Usually it means making a greater effort: working or studying harder or more patiently, breaking up the problem into manageable pieces. It might mean turning to someone for help or advice. Since giving up was not an option for me, it was only a matter of how much work to put into a challenge. It is no naïve belief that everything will work out: hard work actually does pay off. Bette Davis said that for depression, a different kind of challenge, work pays off with the uplift of seeing the results you produce (*Mother Goddam*, Whitney and Davis, W.H. Allen and Co., 1974).

I consciously made myself look at the positive side. For the horrendous performance at my Master's exam, I would retake the oral exam. For the loss of my job, I would start anew in Puerto Rico. And for my failed marriage, in three words, my son Kenny. As all of these difficult experiences molded and matured me, I wouldn't change a thing.

You can make optimism come true by being very purposeful about looking at the positive side of things. When you find yourself in a predicament, neither wallow in self-pity nor waste time on shoulda-coulda-woulda. Instead, figure out what you need *to do* to get through the problem. Some situations are more difficult to overcome than others, but hang in there. I have made the process conscious. There comes a moment when I've worked through the mess and put it in its place to once again move forward with energy just as I did when faced with prejudice as a young girl. In pursuit of success and personal happiness, the driver's seat is mine. No one else is steering for me.

A natural product of optimism is the belief that you can accomplish anything when fiercely committed. There is always a way, but it's up to you to figure out how. The key question is whether the goal is important enough to you to be willing to put in the time and effort. When you are struggling, there comes a moment of truth when you need to ask, "How much do I want this? Am I willing to put in the time and effort it requires?" If the answer is a resounding "Yes," then, yes, you can do it. The most important attributes for success are motivation and a deep personal belief that you can do it. You can be born the most gifted person in the world, but if the motivation and confidence are not there, success may elude you.

Sometimes there are obstacles that seem insurmountable. They could be physical, or social, like racism, or just native intelligence. But then, you hear about people who accomplish amazing things against all odds. Oscar Pistorius, a double amputee, is a world class sprinter. Erik Weihenmayer, a blind man, climbed Mount Everest. Helen Keller? Consider Supreme Court Justice Sonia Sotomayor and the obstacles she had to overcome in her journey from the projects of the South Bronx to the prestige of our high Court. These examples should help you believe you, too, can do it. How important is it to you, and how much are you willing to put into it?

The year 1976 challenged my optimism like no other year. I lost twenty-five pounds within a few months, failed a critical exam, ended a seven-year marriage, became a single parent and lost my teaching job. Yet, six months later I had passed my orals, received my Masters Degree, moved to Puerto Rico and started to teach at the college level. And, good Lord, I was no longer living in government subsidized housing.

A positive attitude and a proactive attitude are intertwined. They form a wonderfully reinforcing cycle. Optimism leads me to believe in my ability to take action, and that ultimately those actions will lead to success. When *stuff* happens, and stuff will happen, the most important thing is how you respond to it, whether you take personal responsibility for making your optimism come true.

The unwelcome opportunity to work this through came from my son when he was a freshman in college—his panicked phone call to my office when he saw his grades. He was in tears as he stared at three F's on his transcript. College was the first time Ken had been away from home, responsible for his own freedom. He had a car and was very popular on campus. I left my office immediately and met him in school, where the Dean probed the reason for the failures. Too difficult? Not working hard enough? Nervously, Ken admitted "Not working hard enough." The Dean was encouraged because, with that reason, there was an easier solution than if Ken had found the work too difficult. And so he outlined the course of action: on probation for the next two semesters and summer school for the next two years, all with a required grade average. My biggest concern was that my son would become a statistic—the drop-out rate for Latinos is one of the highest in the nation. It would have been so easy for Ken to give up and drop out. He had choices. As angry as I was with him that day, I've never been as proud of him as I was of his reaction. He was in a deep hole, yet he never mentioned giving up.

He dug in, he did his work and he pulled himself out of that hole, exactly as I hoped. He went to summer school and achieved the required average. He went back the next semester and still maintained that average. He pulled himself out of probation to graduate with his class. So my approach to my son was exactly the same as to myself: realize your optimism with hard work.

Much later in life, my career was stalled—I had been in essentially the same position for nine years. Granted, I held a prominent position as Vice President of Human Resources for one of the company's businesses, and I understood that promotions become scarcer higher in the organization. As always, I measured my success in relative terms, as more senior positions became available and others were getting them with lesser qualifications. But although I felt stalled, I remained very engaged in the work of my business unit and the company. I was active in the broader Human Resources function. I gave my discretionary energy by participating, volunteering and voicing my opinion. Regardless of disappointments, I would be the best HR lead I could be.

This attitude got the attention of the new head of Corporate Human Resources, who noticed me and became a remarkable mentor. In the course of our dialogues about optimism, Bud Bilanich (motivational speaker, author and blogger; www.budbilanich.com) introduced me to The Optimist Creed. The Optimist International Organization, established in 1971, is a non-profit group that benefits children. We were struck by the similarities of my experience and one of the points of the Creed: "Look at the sunny side of everything and make your optimism come true."

There's a double message here. One is to approach life from a glass half-full perspective, to believe that every experience, good or bad, is movement forward. The second part, 'make your optimism come true,' acknowledges that there's work to be done, the proactive part.

The pessimist doesn't deal constructively with failure; instead he tends to view it as confirmation of his pessimism, whereas the optimist is more likely to ask, "What can I learn from this?" If you are able to gather insights from your successes and failures, the benefits multiply going forward. You build confidence when you understand how your experiences changed you and how they fit in the bigger picture of your life. The ability to incorporate all this consistently is directly related to your level of optimism. Although a painful experience is hardly fun as you experience it, it gives you one more bit of knowledge to help you be successful next time.

UPON REFLECTION,
here are some takeaways to
maintain a positive and proactive attitude:

Look for the opportunities in every situation.

Choose to approach life with optimism. Neither wallow in self-pity nor waste time on shoulda-coulda-woulda. Instead, figure out what you need to do to get through.

Act to make your optimism come true.

Stand by your Personal Integrity

Believing in yourself makes it easy to stand by your principles.

A piece on personal integrity falls under a chapter on Self-Confidence because they feed each other all day long. To remain true to oneself in difficult situations requires conviction and confidence. Conversely, doing the right thing, especially when it's difficult or uncomfortable, bolsters your confidence. Personal integrity and self-confidence reinforce one another in an upward spiral. If you are self-confident, it's easier in some ways to do the right thing because, at your core, you believe in yourself, value yourself and feel good about yourself.

Personal integrity was one of the most important values that our parents ingrained in us. Life was all about the kind of people they strove to be and demanded that their children become. It meant honesty, doing your schoolwork or paying work as well as you could, being dependable and responsible citizens of the community. Personal integrity for our family was intertwined with being a good Christian, living the Ten Commandments and respecting other principles of our religion.

When I was ten, Mom sent me to the *bodega* to buy some spices for dinner, and I happily ran home with the good news that the store owner mistakenly gave me too much change. Not only had I gotten the groceries Mom needed, but I brought back more money than I had started out with. Money was so scarce for us, I thought I had done a good thing, but when my father got home from work, he immediately went to the little market to return the extra money. Needless to say, I was in trouble at home and quite embarrassed that my good thing had converted into a bad thing. The owner of that modest bodega always had a special regard for my father, and on occasions when Pop was strapped for money, credit was no problem. Through experiences like these, my siblings and I were learning the benefits of truth, trust and integrity.

Being on Welfare was an embarrassment to our family. It was a matter of integrity because, for our parents, it was important to earn what you had. We saw how many others, not all, took advantage of Welfare and lied to get more benefits. That is why, as soon as they were able to, our parents pulled themselves out of the program against the advice of the social workers. We were on Welfare for seven long years, and when we walked away from it, our heads were held high.

Integrity played out daily in our school life. We were expected to behave, to be good students. We did our homework and studied hard for exams. We didn't cheat or 'play hooky.' We were rarely absent, as our drill sergeant, Mom, relied on an old theory about school attendance. If you could get out of bed, you were well enough to go to school.

Leaders are presented with many situations where the integrity-confidence loop plays out. Large corporate environments can be highly political, where 'corporate speak' permeates communications and confuses employees about what is really going on. Workers don't even know where to go for the true story. A good leader uses straight talk with employees; gives the tough messages honestly; and demonstrates a desire to improve and develop. A bad leader chooses the easy way out by glossing over important messages and avoiding the direct, tough conversation. In those cases, employees lose out on valuable information, and the leader forever loses integrity and an opportunity to build self-confidence in this challenging area.

My reputation built up for being a straight talker—saying what I meant and meaning what I said. Employees often visited to ask my point of view or solicit feedback because they knew that I would tell them the truth. However, sometimes there was the dilemma of my wanting to say more, not being able to tell all and still being truthful. Most of these situations occurred during organizational restructurings of buying or selling businesses. The certainties of acquisitions are that there will be layoffs, sites will close and entire organizations will be disrupted. Those in positions of responsibility will know certain things that are not for general release to the public or even inside the company. Invariably, rumors will float and employees will ask questions. This situation hit me many times.

How would you respond to an employee who came to you for more information because she had "heard a rumor," and was worried for her job? Let's say that the rumor is true, but you've been told to keep it confidential. Early in my career this situation was an integrity dilemma, as I would not lie any more than breach my boss' confidence. Initially there seemed to be no choice but to be evasive, "I don't know anything about that," and pay the price of feeling that I had done something wrong, that I lacked integrity. With experience, though, and the help of a few outstanding leaders, I learned to tell the truth, that I could not speak about that subject at that point. I would not address a rumor one way or another. But I did assure employees that we would communicate as soon as possible after a decision had been made.

More distressing were situations where an employee would say he had a job opportunity within the company or elsewhere, at a time I knew he was going to lose his job. At times like those, I felt trapped in the gray areas of integrity. In fact, I lived in grays for a long time. Clearly the employee was asking for help, yet I couldn't give him the information he sought. Instead, I focused on the position that he was considering. How did it fit in his career goals? Was it something that he really wanted to do? I tried to get him focused on making the decision for the right reasons and not because of a rumor or fear of what might happen. I always made a personal effort to listen intently and give the best advice I could. Always. There were many times when the employee would say, "I understand you can't talk about it, but thanks for listening." Other times the comment would be, "You really didn't help me very much here." And I was truly sorry.

Over the years, my respect for my responsibility to the organization and to the employees grew. Since a decision is not final until it is final, I would not take it upon myself to convey information that I was not free to communicate. Even when a decision becomes final, it takes time to prepare to communicate it well. Often, these communications mean delivering bad news, so it is key to make sure to communicate it in the right way and with a support structure in place. I would not let anyone experience a cold pink slip in the mail, like my own experience when I was laid off by the Board of Education. It was my good fortune to work for a company that supported this philosophy: when you have to say goodbye, be humane.

It was my privilege to work with many outstanding leaders, but for one who embodies the characteristics of personal integrity, a specific individual comes to mind. He led his organization through dramatic, transformational change resulting from acquisitions, globalization and the changing pharmaceutical industry. His personal commitment to the values held dearly by the company, among which *Integrity* and *Respect for People*, are also prominent. Demonstrating courage, he is true to himself when he reminds senior executives that the tough decisions they have just made will cause a lot of people significant hardship. He stands behind his values even as he notices some uncomfortable shifting in the room. A Canadian setting comes to mind.

One year, we announced the closing of a manufacturing site in Canada. The people of that site had recently launched a campaign reinforcing the values of our company, so we anticipated some tough questions about how values came into play when we were laying off people. Fair enough. This leader believed it was important to make the announcement in person, so that he could address their questions honestly and face to face. And of course, the question expected was the question asked, "How can you say you have respect for people when you are telling us that we are losing our jobs?" The single answer he gave is that we must make the decisions that are right for the business, and we demonstrate respect for people by the way we carry out those decisions: by making the announcement in person, by explaining the reasons, by announcing the decision as early as possible and then by providing generous separation benefits and programs to help employees get back on the job market. We looked for every way we could make the transition as easy as possible, given that business needs made a tough decision necessary.

We did not expect applause, however, there was a level of understanding. Workers don't smile when told that they're losing their job. But having that face-to-face communication, listening to the tough questions and giving thoughtful responses was important to the process.

The Canadian site closed down two years later with an incredible record of accomplishment even during the downsizing process. The employees created an album of photographs and memories to remind them of their accomplishments and the friendships formed during their time with the company. This experience was repeated many times as Pfizer acquired and divested businesses. Not only did I see personal integrity in the leader's behavior, there was tremendous integrity in the way that the employees performed at their best to the very last day.

It takes unusual courage to sustain personal integrity. The leader didn't enjoy giving bad news to a room full of people. It would have been easier to issue a written memo and let local leaders deal with it. But he handled it in person because he was brave and it was the right thing to do.

When my human resources career started in a much smaller pharmaceutical company, it was clear that one of the senior leaders in the company was slated to be the next site manager. Then, news came that he was involved in something morally wrong. It surfaced at a time when I was still learning my role as the head of Human Resources, unsure if it was my job to intervene. I was also frankly scared of the consequences and considered just letting it go. However, I couldn't let it go. So I found a private moment, took a deep breath and spoke with him in the voice of Human Resources. His conduct, I explained without judgment, undermined him as a leader and would threaten his effectiveness when he became the leader of the whole site. His reply left me speechless: "Get with the game, or as soon as I'm Site Director, you're out of here." Ashen and shaken, I went home to think about it. At 28, I didn't know what to do. The next day, I told my boss the whole story, and his look of astonishment and disappointment was unforgettable. With the investigation that followed, the jaded senior leader left the company. A few years later, he contacted me and told me, surprisingly,

that he did not harbor any hard feelings towards me. He had been in a
bad place at that earlier time in his life and had made a mistake. His
candor was honorable. It was gratifying to hear, though my superiors
had backed me at the time, that I had done the right thing even from
that manager's perspective. Once he regained his equilibrium.

Much later in my career, I experienced a similar dilemma of when
to speak out. Our firm was in the midst of integrating two global
businesses, and there were serious issues with our leader to the point
where I thought that the integration was at risk. My peers urged me, in
my role as head of Human Resources: "Do something about it." Now,
complaining about your boss is one of those unspoken taboos,
guaranteed to ruin even an excellent relationship. So I consulted with
my superior and mentor, who also agreed that it was my responsibility
to raise the issue with the head of corporate Human Resources. A
confidential investigation followed, with the leader assigned to another
position. I was assured that my role in the issue was totally confidential
and thanked for doing the right thing. This time, though, the ending
was not as satisfying as the jaded manager example, but taught me a big
lesson in corporate politics.

I remained in the same position for many years. As my applications
for promotions were unsuccessful, I wondered what was going on—I
had solid experience and excellent feedback on my performance. My
bosses supported my candidacy for higher positions and were also
puzzled when the jobs did not come through. One boss finally discovered
the big secret. The 'confidential' do-something-about-it episode was not
kept as confidential as I was told. Indeed, all of senior leadership knew
it and didn't want a Human Resources leader who could 'rat' on them. I
felt betrayed by the organization. I had followed all the rules, had
sought guidance from my superiors and had done as instructed. Due to
an independent investigation that confirmed my observations, upper

management decided on their own to take action, but I was being penalized for doing the right thing. While at times I dwelled on the unfairness of it all, my natural tendency toward optimism kept me focused on being the best Human Resources leader I could be. I was grateful to my boss for telling me the truth, which must not have been easy for him. He demonstrated courage by doing me a great favor, because I had been clueless. Although my career suffered a setback, I knew that I had done the right thing. I would do it all over again. I felt okay with myself.

With the wisdom of introspective hindsight, I have come to treasure all of my extended time in the position. The organization gave me my early developmental experiences as leader of a function and as member of a top leadership team. I learned about running a global business from research to manufacturing to marketing and sales. I experienced firsthand the original global integration in Pfizer's history and learned through direct experience the importance of cultural integration as well as structural integration.

The leadership of a failing business, while not something to be wished on anyone, is a unique opportunity that challenged us to maintain an energized workforce—absolutely critical if we were to come out of it successfully. What exhilaration when we triumphed! Plus the lessons learned about effective and ineffective leadership; how to access corporate resources; about public affairs and the power of great internal communications. Most importantly, I made many long-lasting friendships.

Over time, leaders retire or leave while others join the company. A new HR leader came to Pfizer to lead the function, and soon after I moved to my next job in a larger organization which in turn led to the top Human Resources position in the largest pharmaceutical company in the world.

Personal integrity is being true to self, doing the right thing especially in difficult situations. I learned as a little girl that it's wrong to keep the extra change when a cashier makes a mistake, and it feels so good to make it right. Better than, say, keeping the money ever could. But most importantly, I wanted others to treat me like that store owner treated my father—with exceptional trust. I'm comfortable in my intentions and the role that I played in the last two stories. If you do the right thing, things do tend to work out in the long run. In those rare cases when it doesn't work out, the notion of personal integrity is that you still have the satisfaction of knowing you did your best and you did the right thing.

UPON REFLECTION,
here are some takeaways
to stand by your personal integrity:

Feed your self-confidence directly by living with a strong sense of personal integrity.

Personal integrity is money in the bank. Keep deposits regular; don't deplete the balance; spend it wisely.

Part Four
Performance

Education,
Education, Education

*Education is an indispensable springboard. Personal and
professional success both depend on how you
continue to learn throughout your life.*

A good education beyond high school must give you the
knowledge and facts that are basic to your field—medicine, teaching,
engineering and so on. But the most important benefit of education is
more fundamental: it shapes how you think through issues, analyze
problems and make judgments. The thinking quality these processes
share correlate directly to performance at work. Also, education teaches
you the work ethic that will be necessary to do a good job. A school that
demands a lot from its students prepares them best for life's real
challenges. Finally, college life provides opportunities for social

interactions with people outside of your immediate environment—an experience that will be repeated throughout your work life.

Education was our parents' mantra when we were growing up. It was evident from the beginning, in the one-room country school house where mornings were dedicated to first graders and afternoons to second and third graders combined. When six-year old Waldy started first grade, Mom sent along four and a half year-old Radames because she wanted to give Radames a head start—there was no kindergarten nor any program named Head Start. Mom proudly remembers that the following year, when Radames was officially in first grade, he would complain he had "Already learned that."

As we grew up, my siblings and I understood that our parents wanted to give us the opportunities that circumstances had denied them. Precisely because their economic situation forced them to drop out of school, they were going to do everything possible to keep their own children in school. An education would give us choices they never had. They knew it; we came to know it, too. At times when they would comment how fortunate we were to be in school, we realized with some sadness how much they had wanted to stay in school.

When we moved to New York, the focus on education only intensified. With a new language to learn, we had some catching up to do. Mom saw to it that we stayed focused and disciplined. Picture the five of us sitting around the kitchen table doing our homework—like a Norman Rockwell painting except with *arroz con pollo* on the stove. Although Mom could not help us with the content of our schoolwork, she supervised us like a task master. Our environment stayed silent. Our report cards were scrutinized. And even though our parents did not speak English, down they went to every parent-teacher meeting religiously. We would show our parents to our teachers and then be excused—other parents would translate. Mom and Pop always walked out gleaming with pride. We were good students who usually qualified for the honors programs offered in public schools. Those early years gave us the study habits and the love of learning that lasted a lifetime.

My most urgent message to young people is to stay in school—finish school—no matter what the sacrifice. The time invested may seem long when young, but in a lifetime it is a small investment with enormous payback. A good and complete education never stops giving back. You build on it the rest of your life. But learning cannot stop when you get your last degree. Professional success depends on continuing to learn as an adult. If you are ambitious about building a career, you must be able to climb steep learning curves. You must demonstrate the higher-order cognitive skills of analysis, synthesis and judgment.

Manage your Own Learning

Every job presents unique learning challenges, and you can hardly wait for or expect your superiors to give you the handholding you may prefer. On the contrary, your superiors will be most impressed by how you go about managing your own learning.

My first position in Human Resources put me on a learning curve beyond steep. It was vertical. I did not have the basic knowledge of the function or the industry. The job came my way not for my experience in the field—I had none—but because the leaders were impressed by how quickly I learned and how resourceful I was. They took a chance on me, and I could not let them down. Managers planned to evaluate me based on how quickly I progressed. To begin my education, they gave me the book *Personnel Management* by Chruden and Sherman. It was an old book even then, a textbook that I studied as if preparing for a final exam, underlining key points and writing comments on the margins. I also bombarded my boss, fellow employees and other experts with questions about my new field. There I was essentially managing my learning, creating my own curriculum and setting the pace. It was very different from school, but it was certainly educational.

Much later in my career, on my first big assignment working with overseas markets, another great boss took a big risk on me and gave me responsibilities beyond what I expected. Not long after the position started, one of our overseas businesses submitted a proposal to modify their local employee pension plan. While I knew nothing about structuring pension plans, much less in a country 5,000 miles away, I wanted to have a recommendation ready for the boss by the time he returned from a four-week business trip. Once again, I sought base learning from a book before tackling the proposal. It seemed that every new project turned into a mini-course on another human resources subject. When my boss returned from his trip, I could speak intelligently about the subject, had reviewed the proposal and had prepared an opinion already.

Learning from books has always been a good first step for me, but that is not the case for everyone. We all learn differently, with different learning styles. For example, in the pension plan project, I could have gone to the specialists in the Corporate Benefits group for help in understanding pensions and the proposal we received. Or I could have sought guidance from other peers with more experience in these issues. Knowing your own style is helpful, but what is most important is to be proactive about your learning.

Learn by Teaching

The two years I spent in the Corporate Training and Development Group were intensive. Despite my teaching experience, Train-the-Trainer programs were immensely beneficial for their content knowledge in the field of leadership. As I taught others how to be good leaders, my own skills improved both at work and at home.

For example, to help work teams perform more effectively, we used a personality profiling instrument that gave insights into our behaviors and their impact on others. Then at home when my thirteen-year-old son tried out the questionnaire, his orientation towards socializing showed up to be a result of his extroversion. That clarity made me more patient with him and better able to guide him through important life decisions. Another work program taught problem solving and decision-making skills that helped when I was buying my first house. I patiently explained the decision-making process to my parents to get their input on the house where they too would be living. Smiling, they tried very hard to add their own must-haves and want-to-haves without seeming too demanding.

Sharing my stories with colleagues and 'students' added credibility back to the program. In another of those welcome positive spirals, I would learn a skill so that I could teach it. Then I taught it, applied it to my personal life for a better understanding and applied that insight to be a better teacher. My two years in the Training and Development Group were pivotal to my personal development, teaching me the most about the type of leader I would become.

Learn from Mentors

It has been my good fortune to have mentors throughout my life, each playing a different role, but all giving of their wisdom unselfishly. A high school teacher broadened my goal of a college education. A professor in graduate school expanded my dream of teaching to the college level. My first boss in industry guided my learning of Human Resources. Another man taught me patience when I faced the gender barrier. Many others guided me through the pitfalls of corporate politics. A courageous woman showed me how to be purposeful about talent development.

These mentors held common traits: the ability to extract meaning and lessons from their experiences and a willingness to share their wisdom generously. My mentors acted as hands-on teachers: they helped short-cut the learning process. They uniformly set the tone that made me secure enough asking for their guidance on a new challenge or when I just needed help. It was easy to ask them what I could have done differently or better, trusting in their good intentions towards me.

Learn Especially through Feedback

An athlete uses a coach to enhance her game. No matter the sport, she values an outsider's perspective to help her improve simply because she cannot be herself and see herself at the same time. Each of us has the capacity for outstanding performance, but like the athlete, we need feedback to realize that potential.

As a newly appointed Spanish teacher, I was a little ambivalent about my first experiences being coached. My department head observed me in class periodically, and afterwards we would discuss her observations. I got thumbs up for energy, enthusiasm, lesson plans and class participation, but could do better at getting the students to apply the language. I savored the positive feedback, but cringed at the corrective feedback. I was embarrassed because I did not get straight A's and I was determined to do better. The praise was pleasing, but the negatives in the feedback were less so. Eventually, though, a look back on those feedback sessions showed me how necessary they were to my development as a teacher. How else would I have learned to do something differently? No matter where my strengths, I was blind to my weaknesses. It would have taken me much longer to figure out on my own how I needed to improve. Fortunately, my supervisor was skilled in the art of giving feedback in a way I could hear it without being defensive. By contrast, as an inexperienced Personnel Manager in Puerto Rico, I knew too clearly that I lacked knowledge, so I actively sought coaching from my bosses, locally and in Illinois. These experiences highlight the value of guidance before the fact, followed by feedback after the fact.

My time in Training and Development taught me a lot about giving feedback in a way that the recipient finds acceptable first, then also helpful. Then, my experiences in Human Resources also gave me other insights into the unique dynamics of giving and receiving feedback. Everyone wants to give positive feedback, for the feel-good mood all around. But giving corrective feedback well is a hurdle that only the best leaders overcome. Many leaders—too many—avoid, actually fear, giving corrective feedback. The avoidance comes from lack of confidence in their ability to do it well, and the fear comes from anticipating emotional reactions such as anger or tears. Often, the reticence is from not wanting to hurt the employee's feelings.

On the other side of the feedback loop is the individual who does not want to hear the feedback. Like my early experience with corrective feedback, hearing the flaws of your past or challenges for your future can be a shock. Think of the individual who avoids doctors because he is afraid to find out something is wrong. If he would rather not know, he may thus miss valuable information such as an early diagnosis. So the issue of feedback is two-sided, with the reluctant leader and reluctant employee silently colluding in a sad cycle. It is important to break this cycle because feedback is necessary for personal growth. The outstanding performer will seek feedback for continued development. The great leader will find ways to give constructive feedback.

The most intensive feedback process I experienced was 360-degree feedback. The label comes from the full circle of input collected not only from superiors, but from subordinates and peers alike. When the data is summarized, the strengths and weaknesses tend to emerge clearly. The employee is expected to put together a development plan to improve the more significant areas of challenge. If you participate in the 360 feedback process in your career, you may be anxious about the results. Early on, I viewed the input like grades in school.

One particular experience with 360 feedback challenged me in an unexpected way. I was looking forward to my results, ever so modestly expecting great feedback. But to my surprise, one area was rated low: my peers did not trust me. Now, that goes to the core of my being, to personal integrity, a quality so important I wrote a separate chapter about it. Additionally, a perception of bias on the part of a human resources leader is not a good thing—bad, bad, bad. Impatient to understand why, I meticulously analyzed my report and noticed that the point average was skewed by one low rating out of six - enough to lower the average significantly. I yearned to understand why one individual did not trust me, but the responses were anonymous. There was no way to investigate other than to speak to all my peers without putting anyone on the spot. It would be difficult for any of them to tell me he did not trust me. It would also be hard to hear it, yet I set up individual meetings with each of my peers. My goal was to make it easy for them to give me the feedback I needed for the sake of my own growth.

One of my peers would not look me in the eye when we met. He mumbled, "Everything was great." It seemed he had more to say but could not get the words out, so I tried an indirect approach. I told him that some others had given me feedback about trusting me. Could he help me understand why 'they' would have low trust in me? Immediately he seemed more at ease, and finally said what I needed to hear. "Others might think," that my close friendship with a certain peer biased me in his favor. I had become good friends with that certain peer when we led a global integration jointly. Of course, there was no favoritism towards him from my part—when I spoke with him about it, he laughed out "I wish!" I did not understand how that perception was even created, so I spoke with another peer who I trusted to be straight with me. He thought about it and said, "Well, you two are closely aligned, agreeing with each other in staff meetings most of the time. I don't remember seeing you disagree on anything at all." That is when the light bulb went on. Armed with the feedback, my friend and I saw how easy it would be to fix this issue. We certainly had our strong disagreements in private, but had made sure as co-leaders to solve the issue before we got to a meeting. Instead, we decided to air out our disagreements openly in meetings. I have never worked so hard for feedback.

The episode was a seminar in miniature on the dynamics of feedback:

- ✦ Feedback raises issues where an individual may have a blind spot.
- ✦ Some leaders are fearful of giving sensitive feedback.
- ✦ Leaders can create a safe setting for giving corrective feedback.
- ✦ Specific behavioral examples are critical so the individual can respond with improvements in action.
- ✦ Feedback must be helpful, not hurtful.

As a leader, I tried not to avoid the difficult conversations directed at subordinates or peers. At the same time, I also worked hard seeking and accepting feedback for myself. As stressful as it is to give corrective feedback, skillfully done, it is a precious gift to the individual. Performance does tend to improve when people have specifics to go on. That, in turn, gives the leader more confidence to pursue a similar approach with others. Two keys are timeliness and effectiveness: Feedback is clearest when given at the time of incident, and most successful when given privately and in a fashion that it can be received.

Immerse Yourself in the Joy of Learning

Getting into something new brings great excitement. Part of the excitement comes from the ever-present element of fear when facing the unknown. Big promotions are invigorating in this way. They can be scary because of a steep learning curve, but very energizing at the same time. If you are going up a steep hill, you can slip on that rise—you can slip on a steep learning curve, too. The possibility of failure is there, but the risk also gets the adrenaline flowing. The best learning, the fastest development, occurs when you are willing to take some risk. There is excitement in being in a place like that, a place not totally safe.

You also need to believe in your ability to handle the new situation by trusting the force of your education and experiences, your problem solving and analytical skills, and your ability to learn new things and to manage your learning. Trust that you have the reserve inside to figure out how to get back up when you slip or to stop yourself from slipping in the first place. People who take on risk are confident they will be able to work through the problems that arise. Taking risks always returns me to the defining moment when I realized that I had to depend on myself for inner strength.

My current learning challenge is writing a book of experiences and drawing the inner lessons from them. Thanks to Bud Bilanich who has given me the gift of his knowledge and guidance, this is me and my book. My dreams did not include writing this out. In fact, as a young immigrant girl struggling to get A's in English, it never seemed I could fill a book. Yet here am I once again learning beyond my self-imposed limitations and benefiting from another selfless mentor.

UPON REFLECTION,
here are some takeaways to
Education, Education, Education:

A solid education is your springboard to success. Step out on it often.

If you are a parent, support schoolwork, see the teachers and stay involved; if you are a student, finish school, whatever it takes.

Be proactive in your learning: Impress your superiors with your own resourcefulness.

Learning and teaching boost each other.

Value guidance before the fact and feedback after the fact. Welcome both.

Learning is a life-long process. Keep learning.

Understand the Business and Where You Fit In

All top performers understand the business they are in and how their roles contribute to its success.

I t was not hard to understand, as a teacher, the importance of education and my role in it. My upbringing and my personal passion for education gave me tremendous clarity about the place learning has in our lives and our society.

Joining the pharmaceutical industry, I was thankful for the translation work I had performed in the preceding months. Along with translating policies and procedures, came an understanding of the manufacturing process and of an industry regulated by the Food and

Drug Administration (FDA). There are unique requirements of sterile manufacturing, safety and health regulations and more. These insights were invaluable as promotions eventually put me in charge of Personnel. Because I had learned about the business before I learned about Personnel, my orientation tended towards business operations. I earned my 'degree' in Personnel under the tutelage of line leaders who, not surprisingly, saw Personnel strictly as supporting their business goals. As I viewed my new chosen field from that perspective, too, I learned to articulate the value of my position in terms the line leaders could understand and accept.

Later, when I joined Pfizer in Puerto Rico, I spent time in each of the manufacturing areas, wherever possible working side by side with workers. For example, to understand the unique issues of the third shift, I arrived at 10:00 PM to speak directly with the night supervisors and employees. Soon I was conversant in the new manufacturing processes, the products and the regulations that governed our industry. A side benefit of my visits was the positive employee relations impact; like many others, our employees enjoyed talking about their jobs—a win-win for a new Human Resources professional who wanted to hear it all.

Occasionally, a line leader would question the rationale of personnel requirements that "Took time away from the real business." Explaining the connection was easy since I saw it hands on. Performance management was important to the business, because we all wanted employees who excelled. People all perform best when they understand what is expected of them—job description and objectives; when they know how they are doing—feedback; and when they believe their supervisors care about them—good leadership. I also worked hard to streamline overly bureaucratic, sometimes obscure, personnel procedures.

The crucial lesson from these early experiences was the importance of knowing the business and specifically how my function and position impacted the performance of the business—a prerequisite to outstanding performance.

In Corporate Training and Development, the correlation between our work and the business was less linear. Two training programs had teachings directly related to business success: improving problem-solving and decision-making skills, and supervising people. The leaders who accepted the benefits, 'got it,' brought Training and Development into their organizations to help their supervisors and managers improve leadership skills. Other leaders were skeptical about the value and kept us at arm's length. To my disappointment, too many of the senior leaders of the company kept their distance. Our group remained small and eventually downsized and merged with the business units. My time in this group benefited me tremendously. It was central to my own development as a leader and gave me life-long friends. Nonetheless after two years, I was itching to get back to a business unit.

After sixteen years in the human health business, I moved to a very different industry in Pfizer Animal Health. We made and sold medicines for cattle, pigs, poultry, horses, cats and dogs. The businesses that dealt with such different animals left me immediately confused. To make things more challenging, we had just acquired another company, heading straight into a global integration. This could have been a nightmare experience: a business I did not yet understand, combined with a global integration, an area in which the company had very little experience. I clearly felt the excitement of the potential—for failure.

It was my very good fortune to be working closely with a colleague who had spent his entire career in the animal health industry. He understood the business like few others. As the firm worked through the integration of two sales forces, two distribution systems, two manufacturing organizations, two marketing organizations and two headquarters structures in every country, I was learning about the animal health business itself. My colleague and mentor was patient enough to teach me the business and impatient enough to demand that I learn fast. As the frenzy of the integration died down, learning about the business continued. I spent a full day each alongside cattle, pork, poultry and companion animal sales representatives in Colorado and in North Carolina. I got mud on my shoes in the cattle ranches and manure on my clothes from swishing tails in the dairy barns. I had the unusual opportunity to observe fifty chicken necropsies (animal autopsies), carrying with me the lingering aroma of the innards. By contrast, the swine waste pools were almost a non-event. It was an amazing education into the bowels of the business. After each trip, I would review my insights with my colleague-mentor, who helped me make the connections with other parts of the business.

With every step in my career, there were new aspects of the business to learn. My biggest craving was the need to understand the links between what I did and why we were in business. When my job made sense in the context of the business, it was more energizing and motivating. The reverse situation would have been quite boring to me, a 9-to-5 minimal obligation with the only objective to make money. For me, understanding made for a much richer experience. Being part of the process of providing medicines for people and animals, I made a difference.

This section fits into the chapter on performance because to excel in how you function in your job, you must understand the business that your company is in and exactly how your job impacts that business. If you work in show business, for example, that is a business. If you work for a non-profit, they likewise have goals, focus, organization and purpose of being. As my stories illustrate, there are many ways to achieve this understanding: books, peers, employees, bosses, mentors, training programs and other opportunities that your company offers. They are all there for you if you are proactive about your learning.

UPON REFLECTION,
here are some takeaways to
Understand the Business and Where You Fit In:

To optimize performance, know the full nature of the business and how you contribute to its success. Your credibility is enhanced when you are able to articulate this relationship to yourself and to your superiors.

Understanding makes for a much richer experience than just working your job.

Make it Your Business to Perform

*An outstanding performer is one who consistently
meets and often exceeds expectations.*

My father was the best role model for a strong work ethic. His
green eyes sparkled as he related the compliments he received for the
cleanest floors in the hospital. His focus was on doing work he could
sign his name to, never stopping to consider if the chore was beneath
him. He took pride in doing the best job he could. He could be depended
on to be present, to honor commitments, to meet deadlines and to
follow through. A good work ethic was synonymous with personal
integrity. His humbling example has endured within our family.

A good work ethic forms a foundation, the prerequisite to good
performance. Over the years, working with colleagues who live out this

value makes for a delight, where mutual trust and respect grew very quickly. When trust is high and motivation is high, performance is optimal and the day is a joy.

Be a Self-Starter—Take Action

My training as a teacher taught me to think proactively about ways to help my students learn, confident I knew the subject matter and how people learn. When I entered the world of Human Resources in the pharmaceutical industry, I scrambled to figure out how to succeed in this new world. One manager went out of his way to help me make the transition successfully. He was a straight talker I could count on to be painfully blunt but helpful in his feedback—a unique mentor. It was his coaching that taught me how to take charge of my own learning.

Over time, I learned that the most successful employees are those who, having clarity in their role and in the business, will figure out what needs to be done and how to do it. This is the same quality as managing your own learning, good news for anyone who is action-oriented, an intrinsic quality addressed in *Maintain a positive and proactive attitude*. My bias towards action comes from a deep-seated belief in myself, that I can take risks and face challenges even when a positive outcome is hardly guaranteed.

Within months of making the career change, I faced a great challenge, to draft an Affirmative Action Plan (AAP) for my company. Part of the challenge: I had no idea what an AAP was, and my line colleagues could not help much because it is very specialized human resources work. Companies are required to analyze their work force demographics in comparison to the external environment, and address any inconsistencies regarding women or minorities. I was expected to develop the AAP locally and then submit it to headquarters in Illinois for review. This requirement felt like taking a final exam after missing a set of key lectures. I considered begging forgiveness this time around because I was new to the company and the function, requesting an expert from headquarters to come to our site. But that would be letting down the leaders who took a chance on me. And so I committed to doing the AAP, heaven help me.

The biggest challenge of the AAP was a statistical analysis based on eight factors defined by the federal government. Thank goodness numbers are my friends; still, it was slow and meticulous work. Federal guidelines were not as detailed as I would have wanted, but one step at a time, and each day brought some progress until finally it was done. I submitted the plan to corporate headquarters before the due date and then waited. Had I done the right thing by doing it myself? My boss had put his signature on it, which could have been embarrassing. The wait was nerve-wracking, but finally we got the anticipated memo. Not only was our plan approved, but we were complimented on the quality of the document and especially for taking on the challenge of the eight-factor analysis. My boss' proud smile made it all worthwhile. And what an incredibly intense and satisfying learning experience it had been for me. Because I sweated every word, every number, every commitment, I learned a tremendous amount about Equal Employment legislation and regulatory requirements, an important specialty in my new field. This episode of over thirty years ago remains clear because it was my first big win in industry. From then on, the folks far away in Illinois thought of me more as a colleague than a trainee. A maturing event gave me stature.

Present Yourself as the Energizer Bunny

I learned very early that a high energy level is necessary for success in any career. Employers understandably want dynamism, enthusiasm, spirit and vitality in their organization and this is what energy is all about.

One of the first seminars I attended as an HR professional taught interviewing skills. We learned about qualities to assess in an interview and how to evaluate them during a thirty-minute conversation. Playing psychologist made me nervous, but grew into one of the fundamental learning experiences of my career. The focus was on the behavior we could actually observe in the candidate during the interview. It took some practice to see what was right before my eyes. One of the primary qualities we had to assess was 'energy level.' We learned to probe candidates about work and personal experiences that illustrated high energy levels, but most importantly we learned to observe the energy level in the candidate as she spoke—pace of speaking, arm and body movement, expressiveness, enthusiasm. Equally important, we learned to see lack of energy—lethargy, lack of focus, even yawning.

The good news about energy is that it is within your control. Undoubtedly, hard work is fundamental, but the fuel for hard work comes from being in good health from living a healthy lifestyle and maintaining a positive and proactive attitude, qualities addressed in detail in this book. The drive to work hard at whatever you do is rooted in your sense of personal dignity and belief in yourself.

Throughout my career, I have received reinforcing feedback about my seemingly bottomless source of energy. One very intense year, my colleagues referred to me as the 'Energizer Bunny,' going so far as putting the sobriquet on a name plate for my desk. It was quite the compliment, since they, too, were working incredibly hard that year, but knew they could count on me to 'keep on going' when others called it a day. A high energy level became one of my defining leadership traits and my proudest.

Be Known for Flawless Execution

Former colleagues will be disappointed if I do not talk about flawless execution. I often preached to my team about its importance, and occasionally they would accuse me of being unrealistic, of wanting perfection. Perfection was not what I expected, but I was adamant that our senior leaders be able to count on us to follow through.

A document with careless mistakes leaves a bad impression. Individuals who turn in shoddy work quickly lose the trust of superiors and peers. Credibility is a precious asset that takes time to build, but can crumble very quickly because of carelessness. Avoidable mistakes, the kind that can be detected by carefully reviewing work, are caught by double- and triple-checking before submitting it. Employees who take pride in their work make an impact through their work product; they go the extra mile to make sure their work is accurate, that the facts are correct. They deserve the most challenging, and therefore developmental, assignments.

Leaders must be able to count on their organization to follow through on agreed strategies and plans. The best performer is the one who can be depended on to deliver on commitments, to set actions and contingencies in place so that the end result is as expected.

Overcome Fears and Tackle the Tough Problems

A secret quality of a strong performer is the willingness to take on goals in hardship, when the outcome of the goal is also uncertain. My own performance is best in these situations. With the butterflies in my stomach also comes the adrenaline rush, the energy that helps me think more creatively. Giving up or succumbing to fear is not an option. The more frightening a particular goal, the more energy and focus I put into it to overcome that fear. Fear, if kept under control, is good as long as you do not let it paralyze you.

A defining moment for me occurred in ninth grade. We were in a school-wide event in the auditorium, and the classmate who was to introduce the band developed laryngitis. Asked to fill in at the last minute, I was horrified. Public speaking was my worst fear, but telling the teachers I was scared? Still worse. As I walked to the microphone on center stage, it was all I could do to stop my knees from buckling. Hands cold and clammy, heart racing, I opened my mouth and out came nothing. I tried again but heard only a croaking sound. The teacher walked me off the stage and introduced the band herself. I had failed spectacularly, in the most public and humiliating way, in front of my peers and my teachers. The merciless teasing would not have disappointed the most ardent masochist. The kids relished my public failure especially because this straight A student seemed to do no wrong. It was such a mortifying experience that it could never happen again, launching a personal goal to overcome my fear of public speaking. More about this in a subsequent chapter, but say I worked on this most challenging goal for many years until I succeeded. A senior leader must be able to speak in front of large groups, which I did successfully. With the cushion of time and the sharpness of hindsight, I can almost look back on that horrible day without wincing. Almost.

This embarrassment was a defining moment for a number of reasons. First, it was so humiliating that recovery should not have been possible, yet no one died. The sun even came out the next day. A few months later, I graduated valedictorian. Then, the experience gave me the motivation to do something about it. Lastly, overcoming that fear added to my confidence that I could do anything I set out to do as long as I was willing to work hard enough for it.

In a ninth grade auditorium, fear did paralyze me. The experience forced me to face it and make changes. So, even if you do fail, there is always another day and another chance to succeed. If not for working on my fear of public speaking, I would have died a different kind of death. It would have eaten away at who I am. It would have eroded me. To face and overcome the fear of public speaking was important to my self esteem. If you never act on your fears, if you let fear always paralyze you, first you deprive yourself of the chance to succeed, since you very well may succeed. Second, you may be creating a hole inside yourself that just keeps getting bigger, as you walk away from things instead of trying. Not trying is a really dangerous thing, not only from a career perspective, but from the perspective of your self-esteem and your whole life.

As an adult, whenever a particular challenge or goal frightened me, my reaction was predictable: I'll do it!

My first trip to Europe brought adventure *and* challenge. At the last minute, my managers chose me as a substitute to present back-to-back programs to Pfizer scientists in Sandwich, England. Planning my trip, I asked my colleague how he got from London to Sandwich. He casually responded that he rented a car, but the idea scared the daylights out of me. However, if he could do it, why couldn't I? If I flew to London, I could drive to the hotel in Canterbury. I was very nervous about driving in England on the other side of the road, but I was not going to admit that.

There was no way to anticipate how tiring an overnight flight plus jet lag would be. But the excitement of the adventure had begun, and the adrenaline was flowing. After picking up my rental car, with map in hand, I drove into London traffic—both hands were white from gripping the steering wheel so hard. All my instincts told me to stay on my side of the road, to drive on the right. Afraid that habit would prevail and have me end up in a head-on collision, I started talking to myself, "Stay to the left. Stay to the left."

In the outskirts of London, I had to ask for directions from a friendly 'lorry' driver. Both the truck driver's explanation and Cockney accent were impossible for me to decipher even after he repeated them several times, but thanking him graciously, I drove in the general direction he showed me. The highway headed east and my car settled into the slow lane on the right for a quiet one-hour drive. Drivers flashed their headlights at me for some reason before they passed me in the left lane. Only later did I learn the right lane is the fast lane, explaining why local motorists were not happy with me.

By mistake, I took a wrong turn off the highway and ended up in the center of a small town with no one in sight. There was parking in front of an office building, and I entered an architect's office on the first floor. He was kind, pulling out a street map and giving me detailed directions back to the highway. When I finally got off the highway at the right exit, I drove on local roads for a while. Staying to the left of a too-narrow country road was downright scary, as cars whizzed close by and my inner commands increased in urgency: "Stay left! Stay left!" When I reached the hotel, I breathed a sigh of relief—a one hour drive had taken me two hours, and still I was euphoric for the success mixed with terror the entire way.

The program participants I met were quite impressed with my bravery to drive in England on my first visit. They were encouraged to suggest other 'brave' adventures, which of course I pursued with a sense of excitement. The conservative plan to fly to Brussels that weekend turned into a ferry ride across the English Channel to Calais, France and then a car ride into Paris for a weekend of touring. From Paris, on to Brussels via train. After a day in the office, I walked the city and took the train from Brussels to Bruges, a beautiful Venice-like city.

Thirty-three years old and this was my first trip across the Atlantic. I drove on the left side of the road in England and toured Canterbury, Paris, Brussels and Bruges. Despite my fragile nerves, the English, the French and the Belgians were all very helpful, even when language was a problem. This experience gave me the confidence for many years of solo travel around the world.

There were many times in my career when my team and I faced

enormous challenges. I can still see my colleagues playfully rolling their eyes as I enthusiastically explained what fun it would be to figure out the challenge. It was actually the toughest goals that produced the most invigorating thrill.

My new husband teases me for seeking this thrill even in my personal life. We go on an annual wilderness trip of canoeing and portaging—hiking and carrying heavy backpacks. The trip is rigorous, during which we challenge ourselves physically by the distance we cover and the difficulty of the trails. O.B. complains if I do not stop to smell the roses for the rush to make the next milestone. Often he is right—he will not let me pass those roses without smelling them. Every year we adventure out, we do not know how the weather will treat us, how rigorous the trails will be or how shallow the rivers. One year we made the trip in late September, a cold and wet trip. The foliage was spectacular, but it was a challenge to stay warm. At the end of the trip, the adrenaline was flowing and we felt powerful.

That powerful feeling is the one that only comes when you have challenged yourself to go beyond your self-imposed limits. The outstanding performer imparts energy, manages his learning, sets courageous goals, has the confidence to take risks and learns from successes and mistakes. May you have many of each.

UPON REFLECTION,
here are some takeaways to
Make it Your Business to Perform:

Take personal pride in doing the best job possible, whatever the job.

For success in any career, show employers dynamism,
enthusiasm, spirit and energy.

Figure out what needs to be done, plan out how to do it, then do it;
do not wait for the assurance that the outcome will be guaranteed.

Take the time to build credibility; guard credibility against
crumbling quickly due to careless flaws.

Not trying is more dangerous than failing. Accept your fears with
fascination. Do not let them paralyze you.

Watch the toughest goals produce the most invigorating thrill.

Part Five

Organizational Savvy

Pick Up
Organizational
Savvy

In every organization, there exists a labyrinth of relationships or
historical connections that explain a lot about how people get along.

This chapter could have been named Organizational Politics, but playing politics has negative connotations around the world and in 'office politics' in particular. Describe someone as political, and you hint at someone who pursues his agenda to benefit himself, maybe even to the detriment of others or the organization. There are people like that, but most employees simply want to understand how to be successful.

Read Between the Lines

Organizational savvy is all about understanding the unwritten rules at work: perceiving the nuances that define appropriate behavior and grasping the meaning between the lines. People with superior observation and interpersonal skills have an edge in the pursuit of career success. They notice and apply the unique ways the organization gets things done. They listen to what people say, but also observe what they do. They partner well with different kinds of people at all levels of the organization.

When I changed companies early in my career, adjusting to my new company took time. I missed the familiarity of my former company, the people and knowing the ins and outs of how work got done. My new company had one thick manual of policies and another of job descriptions, but there was nothing to describe the unwritten norms of how people were expected to behave. Study the norms or there is no understanding your company's culture.

The issues that arise when people step into different cultures crystallized during my first experience at integrating an acquired business. We appointed some leaders to very senior positions in the new company and watched how bewildered they were trying to learn the ropes. Recalling my own transition to a new culture as a little girl and the move to a new company as a young woman, I admired the managers who made the transition successfully. One of the new appointees seemed to navigate the rough waters of integration better than most, well worth studying. The first thing I observed was that he was rarely the first one to speak in meetings. He listened first, and when he spoke, he asked a lot of questions. Initially, he did not challenge the way things were done in the new company. Then I observed that he sought guidance from the people who reported to him, who had experience at the acquiring company, his new company. He depended on them to help him avoid any faux pas, to tread lightly near sacred cows and to paint in the history that explained confusing behaviors or policies. He was patient and did not rely on assumptions, but when he made a mistake, he was quick to apologize. Last, he methodically reached out to other senior leaders in the organization. He proved to be a very successful leader in the company and years later became my boss.

At the same time, a leader from the acquired company who was also appointed to a senior position was neither very observant nor respectful of the way things were done in our older company. He quickly committed a number of cultural errors that caused friction with a well-respected leader of our organization. Instead of pulling back and trying to understand what was happening, he pushed harder, insisting that his way was better. He was unlikely to win respect that way, and in spite of counseling, he continued to commit one mistake after another. Soon he was no longer with the company.

Whether you join an organization early or late in your career, make it your business to learn the subtleties of the new culture thoroughly. One way to do that is to quietly observe the people who are successful in the organization. How do they dress? How do they conduct themselves in meetings and at social events? What hours do they keep? Do meetings begin on time? Do important communications happen face-to-face, on the phone or via email? How polite are people with each other? How formal or informal? How is talent valued and managed? You can see why good observation, listening and relationship skills are necessary for success.

Make Friends, Build Relationships and Use Your Network

If you join an organization where people have worked a long time, they have the advantage of time. There are relationships or historical connections in place that may seem like an impenetrable web. But if you are purposeful about weaving your way into new contacts, you can accelerate the journey to the core, to be one of the people inside that web of connections.

Begin by establishing the most positive relationships with the people in your immediate group, those you meet on a regular basis. With people outside that group, be more persistent and strategic about building relationships. Introduce yourself and stay in their line of sight on a regular basis, so they remember you when opportunities arise. This is networking: meeting people, introducing yourself, making contacts, making connections, exchanging ideas, hearing people out, interacting and remembering the interaction.

As a young professional, I understood nothing but being the best performer I could be within my organization. Yet, the single biggest mistake people make in trying to manage their career is assuming that if they do a good job in their current position, they are guaranteed to move forward. Good performance helped me get to a certain point and no further. Other talents come into play in career success, and one is whether the people who are making the decisions know who you are. Do not depend on chance to bring you in contact with the decision makers—make it happen. It took me years to catch on.

The best networker I knew was also one of my bosses. He had built his career in another part of the company and when appointed to head our group, he made it his business to remain visible in the broader organization. Two or three times a week, he scheduled meetings with senior leaders throughout the company. He used these meetings to stay informed of what was going on outside our group, to stay current with senior leaders and to put forward his most talented people for opportunities in other divisions. Most impressively, in social events this leader seemed to know everyone and, not surprisingly, they knew him.

He had excellent social skills and showed genuine interest in everyone—a personally-inclusive leader who made friendships and built relationships with people in different business units. Clearly, those skills were an important factor in his career growth.

Key relationships may also be developed by working in different parts of the business, whether through internships, horizontal moves or appointments. Even without promotions per se, I benefited from a career path that advanced me through most of the divisions in the company. Those experiences not only helped me learn about the business, but also introduced me to a lot of people who moved up ahead of me and who later sponsored me. Some companies like IBM and General Electric have talent development policies that deliberately move people throughout the company to accelerate their understanding of the business and their own professional growth. By the time an employee is a senior leader, she knows all about the business and the people from the ground up and is respected for just those experiences of cross-training.

My early time in the Corporate Training and Development group was also an excellent way to meet people from all parts of the company. Relationships grew with people who I otherwise would not have met, relationships that later helped me move ahead. Furthermore, spending time in a corporate group was a great way to get to know the business more broadly.

Networking can also be accelerated by participating in cross-divisional teams, where you meet people from other business units and have the chance to show your best skills. A good leader will encourage you to participate across divisions to help give you exposure. She does so knowing she risks losing the best people to other units, but willing to give up talent in order to attract talent. I expected people in my HR groups to participate in at least one cross-divisional team so that they would get known. With many project teams that offered the opportunity, there was no excuse for not participating in at least one of them. If the team was of high importance to the organization, people got a lot of visibility. But even teams with lower importance provided some opportunity for added exposure.

There is also the direct approach to networking. Occasionally, young employees I did not know would ask to meet with me, a senior leader. Part of their agenda was introducing themselves to me; another was to ask for mentoring. The system worked, because later I would remember them when opportunities arose or when management held talent development discussions. In that way, approaching a senior leader in a request for a mentoring relationship has two positives: you can learn from that senior leader, and that leader can keep you in mind as opportunities arise.

Use Informal Power

Organizational savvy is also about understanding that work relationships are more complex than any diagram on a company chart can show. There are the people the organization says are in charge, the names in the top boxes. And there are people who have the power, not necessarily the same names. All senior executives have their trusted advisers who, with or without filling senior positions, are quite influential. A junior employee as well as a leader needs to understand who carries formal and informal power, so he can work up positive relationships with both in order to do his job and eventually progress his career.

Digesting the importance of networking, I began reaching out to HR leaders in other divisions, and I became a regular in cross-divisional teams. In each assignment to a different unit, I would spend the first 90 days meeting with the leaders and listening, to understand their issues and their agendas. That was my strategy, listening, as a way of accelerating my knowledge of the unwritten dynamics in that group, as well as defining what my role should be in supporting that business.

Some groups were harder to penetrate than others. In those cases, it took more patience and tenacity, building relationships with the people on the margins who had access to the insiders. Slowly, I would chip my way closer to the most influential leaders. Then I would find the opportunity to demonstrate my interactive skills, my knowledge and experience. Like anyone else, you may be limited by how much you can do, but there is nothing to stop you from presenting yourself in the best light when you do actually come in contact with the insiders.

For years it seemed that all political games had twists I did not want to play. But it was naïve of me to try to ignore the complexities of getting along in the modern organizational life. Organizational savvy is a critical set of skills for anyone who is ambitious about building a career in a company where, for example, other people work.

UPON REFLECTION,
here are some takeaways to
Pick up Organizational Savvy:

In addition to consistently good performance, career success depends on understanding the inner workings of your organization. Study the unwritten dynamics of the group.

How do others act? Good observation, listening and relationship skills are critical. Watch and learn.

Understand who holds the power and be proactive about networking.

Do not depend on luck to be known to the decision makers—make it happen yourself.

Part Six

Now Presenting
...You

Take Care of Your Physical Well-Being

A healthy person is more engaging, creative, energetic and fun.
A healthy person is a better performer.

Unlike school, where your final grade is a direct result of your grades on exams and papers, professional success is the result of many intangible dynamics. Good performance alone is not enough. Therefore, beyond the ways already addressed that showed that actually doing the work directly influences career growth, I took note of who got promoted, who got the high profile assignments. Such eye-openers helped me appreciate the importance of how others experienced me. All of me—what they see, understand and guess accurately or not. Those others encompassed my superiors, peers, subordinates and just about anyone in the course of my workday. I became more deliberate about presenting myself in the best light.

This section focuses on three major areas that are critical for optimizing your presentation of self: health, dress and communication.

Look After Your Good Health

Good health is one of those irrefutable win-wins. We all want to be healthy so that we can enjoy a long and happy life. Our employer wants us to be healthy so that we can perform at our best. When you are healthy, you have more energy to do your job, and you appear differently to other people; you present yourself better; you exude an inviting presence; your skin glows; your eyes are brighter; you are optimistic, positive and more alert. People naturally enjoy being around people like that. They react positively to you.

But, as we all know, staying healthy is a lot of work. It demands purposeful management of life-long habits like smoking, drinking, eating, exercising, managing stress, getting preventive checkups, avoiding addictions and more. Because this chapter on health targets the issues experienced personally, it is not meant to be all inclusive. For example, never smoking or drinking alcohol excessively leaves me with no specifics to offer, but these are important health and social issues that definitely impact performance, career success and, of course, your whole life. Friends have passed from the results of many years of smoking. Careers derailed before my eyes as a result of too many martinis or highs. If these are your issues, they should be the first you address. I pray that you take charge of those top priorities first.

Get Any Exercise That You Enjoy

My siblings and I were fortunate that, aside from childhood illnesses soon after our move to New York, we were essentially healthy kids growing up. And like all young people, we were going to live forever. I was never very physically active—the mandatory gymnastics class was all the exercise I got—but in my early thirties, it hit me like the vast majority of humanity that I was not going to live forever. I was pretty much on schedule as far as accepting my mortality.

In the early 1980's, the United States was in the midst of the running and exercise craze set off by James Fixx's *Complete Book of Running*. Everywhere, there was some article or book about the cardiovascular benefits of running and exercise, and at 32 years old, I was thin as a reed and totally out of shape. With a family history of high blood pressure, my heart health was important for me to improve, so with everyone running, I decided to start running.

At first, my poor physical condition limited me to running in place for two minutes. At the end of two minutes I was exhausted. But I'm nothing if not persistent. Two minutes running in place in my bedroom soon expanded to five minutes around the block. In Terre Haute, Indiana, where I led a supervisory training program, many of the participants were runners and asked me to join them for a run after class. Boasting a ten-minute run got me some friendly banter, but they encouraged me to join them. After the ten minutes, I was winded and they kept going. That week stretched my time to fifteen minutes.

Within a few months, my jogging hit three miles in thirty minutes, seven days a week. No marathoner, I was making progress toward the goal of cardiovascular fitness, and the runs at the end of each day were very enjoyable. I had been running for three years when my knees and ankles began to swell after each run—the frequent pounding was taking a toll on my joints. If I continued to run that way, I would be a candidate for knee replacements before age forty. I was terribly discouraged at the thought of ending such an enjoyable activity, but the original goal—cardiovascular fitness—allowed for other ways to achieve that goal. I joined a gym and used machines and equipment for my aerobic workout. Soon after, Pfizer opened an in-house fitness center, which settled me into an early morning routine.

As daily exercise became an integral part of my life, there were further benefits: nights of deep sleep, mornings waking up fully rested with less effort to focus and days feeling invigorated for anything. It was easier to manage my weight, and colds came less often. Better than a facial, my skin was clearer.

Eat Right and Watch your Weight

I was raised on a Puerto Rican diet—rice, beans, chicken and pork, lots of fried vegetables and starches, richly seasoned sauces. One reason for other bad eating habits was being one of those insufferable people who could eat anything without gaining weight. I was five feet three inches tall and one hundred and ten pounds when I got married, but my pregnancy changed that. Not only did I leave the hospital with an extra fifteen pounds and a bouncing baby boy, but I quickly ate my way to yet another ten pounds. I had never had to deal with weight control much less weight loss. However, six years later, during the very stressful year when I failed my orals, got divorced, lost my teaching job and left New York, I lost the twenty five pounds within months. That was not exactly the recommended regimen for losing weight, but it did give me the incentive to keep the weight off. That is when I got serious about eating right, focusing mostly on portion control. Cold turkey is not my idea of changing a habit.

Changing my eating routine was not easy, but as with running, slowly over time I developed good habits. For example, I used to drink my morning *café con leche* with three teaspoons of sugar—delicious. When I eliminated the milk and sugar, I discovered I really did not like coffee, just the hot milk and sugar. To re-educate my taste buds slowly, the next day I had my café con leche with *only* two and a half spoons of sugar instead of three. The difference in taste was tolerable enough to do that for a couple of weeks. Then the sugar dropped to two teaspoons, then one teaspoon, half teaspoon and the big day finally came for my *café con leche* without sugar. It took about three months to get to that point, but my taste buds had adjusted. I could actually enjoy coffee without sugar. Later I eliminated the *leche*, too, through increments— slowly, steadily, methodically—always keeping the goal in mind.

Notwithstanding what dieticians recommend, my most important meal is dinner, not breakfast. If I could look forward to the enjoyment of dinner, I had the will power to manage my calories during the day. Over time, I reduced breakfast and lunch meals to give me more flexibility for dinner. The method of incremental improvements works for me, although friends successfully manage their weight on other diet plans and exercise regimens. My belief is there is no fixed target weight for each height, because people have unique weights where they feel and look their best.

Schedule Checkups

Twice, my doctors have caught a health problem early enough to treat it successfully. Thanks to those early detections and being consistent about annual checkups and diagnostics, I have no serious health issues.

One day in my early forties, while checking messages in the office, my heart skipped a beat at the calm voice of my gynecologist's assistant asking me to call as soon as possible. The dreaded words 'positive Pap test' got my attention. A dozen dreadful scenarios shot through my mind immediately, all the while wondering how much time there was to update my will. It was an early case of cervical dysplasia, abnormal cells on the uterine cervix that could become cancerous. The malady generally has no symptoms, so most women who have the condition do not know it. After a confirming biopsy, my doctor performed a simple procedure that removed the layer of abnormal cells. That was twenty long years ago.

Five years after that, my annual physical revealed hypothyroidism. Again, no symptoms. A minimum dosage of the standard thyroid medication took care of the problem. That was fifteen years ago. I was very fortunate for the early detection, because I have witnessed the serious harm that a thyroid gone awry has wrought on others, and my annual physicals saved me from experiencing them.

It just makes good sense to take advantage of the technology available to maintain your quality of life. The benefits of early detection are that I can either do something about the issue or, as a realist, I can plan accordingly. "I'd rather not know" is not my segment of the population. Although life has no guarantees, you can be more confident that a major health issue will be caught early if you allow for an annual checkup. You might even want to schedule one today for next month.

Balance Your Life, Manage Your Stress

The best protection against the ravages of extended stress is to lead as healthy and balanced a life as you can. I learned about stress when I taught a workshop on stress management. The first lesson was that stress is part of life and, indeed, you know how a tough challenge entices me. As stage-fright serves to help some, an adrenaline rush bestows a certain acceleration that is actually helpful to the task. It allows me to focus and think better, which is most rewarding for success under those circumstances. This energy boost is the result of the fight-or-flight physical response that helped our ancestors survive real dangers. But that response was meant for short bursts of powerful action. When the body is subjected to long periods of physical changes from the stress response, the body fights itself and many things go wrong.

144

At some point when stress is prolonged, stress can cross the line into distress and becomes harder to reverse. Be attuned to when life situations are challenging and positive and when they are not. Get to know your body well, because everyone has a different threshold where a healthy challenge blossoms into unhealthy distress. Extended distress is insidious in that it homes in on your genetic weaknesses, different for each of us, and you are dealing with high blood pressure, ulcers, insomnia, headaches, distraction or a myriad of other maladies.

There are many sources of distress to our personal lives: illness and death, an unhappy marriage, unemployment, relocation, school, etc. Yet for many in the business world, a common source of distress is long-term imbalance between personal and work lives. We expand our workday and our workweek for different reasons. Dedicated to our work and our clients, we don't want to let anybody down. We believe a very heavy work load is necessary to advance our careers. Since our clients, our bosses and our peers maintain it, we do not want to be seen as less committed. Surely people who are successful in any field are those who are willing to work extremely hard and sacrifice their personal lives. This is the primary way to compete, to set yourself apart. Part of the reason for success in my career was the willingness to sacrifice much of my personal life for work. Luckily, the sacrifices worked because I stayed healthy, I was single and I had great parents looking after my son. Above all, I loved my job and the challenges that came with it. Nonetheless, there were times of struggle to attain personal balance.

The first six months after each new appointment, I had no life-work balance at all. I worked days and nights and weekends. If there were other parts of the week, I would have worked those, too. No surprise there, with a steep learning curve and great things to accomplish in a short time. Each new position had its big challenges like learning the business and the content of the job, plus more travel. I was willing to sacrifice much of my personal life for career success. My overseas trips were often a month long, and upon my return, I was jet-lagged and exhausted. I would fly on weekends so that I could be in a client's office on Monday morning, Sunday morning for an Islamic country. Only, I traveled so much that my parents and my family never counted on me to be present at major family gatherings.

Very lonely, I called home from my Stockholm hotel one Thursday when my family was sitting for Thanksgiving dinner. Down in the lobby, there was an American businessman, and we wished each other "Happy Thanksgiving." Traveling over the four-day holiday weekend was my own choice, but the sacrifice seemed to make perfect sense since they were the only days our office in Sweden was available. When I got back to my office, I realized that this large sacrifice in my personal life had gone unnoticed. Work life went on as usual.

Then was it worthwhile? Although it was my decision to travel on Thanksgiving, I should have scheduled it for a later date. The trip took a toll on my personal life as a lack of balance between home and work. I would never have advertised the effort as a sacrifice, but would have felt better if anyone had noticed. My boss knew all about my trips—at minimum by approving expense reports, but more notably through my trip reports, which summarized objectives and accomplishments of each mission. Thanksgiving, in hindsight, may have been a mistake, certainly never to be repeated.

Between travels, my norm was to get home late in the evening. There were times I would work seven days straight, barely getting four hours of sleep before heading back to the office. In one such routine during a global integration in 1995, I was newly appointed Vice President, excited and energized by the integration. I was learning major new areas: two new businesses; new organizational structures;

the cultural issues of integrations; and the succeeding tough staffing decisions of those integrations. It was a bracing time—the most memorable time in my professional life.

But I did pay a high price: my family rarely saw me, traveling eighty percent of the time for the better part of the year. I skipped going to the gym. After a while, the family stopped making plans around my availability. If I was able to make it, great; if not, life went on without me. While my family did not try to exclude me, they essentially assumed I would be unavailable and went on with their plans. What bothered me was how important my family was to me, but I was not demonstrating any such thing. My personal life was shot, and all I could do was feel guilty about it. Mom and Pop were raising my son—even when I was home, exhaustion made me little more than a casual participant.

The biggest invasion to life/work balance was the pervading email culture that developed in the late 1990's. Expectations about response time changed dramatically from days to hours or even minutes, as the inbox grew and grew. Desktops changed to laptops very quickly, so that we could catch up on email at home.

My social life was also suffering. I had been dating the man who many years later would become my husband. It was a long-distance relationship, with periods when we did not see each other for months and barely had time for short phone calls. It is a testament to our love and his patience that our relationship survived such an extended period of minimal communication. I made those tradeoffs for career success, yet, although I was doing very well, the rewards were not commensurate with the sacrifice. Somewhat underappreciated, I felt at time I was being taken for granted. Some colleagues were equally successful while having a fuller life. When there came a time that the sacrifices made me uncomfortable, I became more purposeful about personal equilibrium, but getting back to a healthier balance was not easy. Like giving up sugar in my coffee, I would not decide to be balanced suddenly as of tomorrow. Expecting unflawed balance every single day is an unattainable goal that would simply add its own stress to my life. During some periods, work demanded more than usual—during an acquisition, a restructuring or a new job. At other times, life away from work had the stronger pull—for a school emergency, an aging parent or a big family event. However, neither pull continued indefinitely, even if that belief needed some repeating.

Given the realities of corporate life and my own career ambitions, the pressures of personal imbalance were to remain a constant companion guiding me to focus on the skills that would best help me cope. The first step was to do a better job of managing my workload. To that end, I had to be more disciplined about setting priorities, managing my time and letting go of doing everything myself.

I had to wean myself off the anti-health treadmill I found myself, especially working on email from home every evening, a difficult habit to break. Instead of taking home my computer seven days a week, I started leaving it in the office one night a week and limiting my on-line time on Sundays and holidays. That slow process was interrupted by the arrival of the Blackberry, which managed to rope me back into my 24/7 connection to work life. Accelerating the process though was the birth of my grandson and three years later my granddaughter. Friday night quickly became that special time with the grandkids and as a result total email silence. It took years before I could stay away from email for a number of weekday evenings. Given my growing responsibilities and the email culture at Pfizer, that detachment was the most that could be expected, but feeling more in control of the choices, I experienced less distress.

As a second step, I made sure to continue leading a healthy lifestyle. A strong, healthy body is better able to withstand stress. Working for a company that invested in the health of its employees made it easier for me to sustain a daily exercise regime. Our medical plan paid for annual physicals, and our cafeteria offered healthy meal alternatives to the usual fare of burgers and fries. Many companies have programs that support employee health, because after all it is humane and also good business. Healthy employees are better performers and more loyal. I urge every employee to take advantage of the opportunities that companies provide towards these goals. As a seasoned HR professional, I also recommend that companies provide such programs to help their employees stay healthy, balanced and productive.

Finally, I learned the benefits of telling others about my aims. Because I tended to work eighteen hours a day, people came to expect eighteen hours a day. Early in the 1990's, before the email tsunami, I included a goal in my personal development objectives to get out of the office by 5:00 o'clock every day. So I was already working on personal balance in my early 40's, albeit with little success. Sharing my goals with others had two big benefits: I learned my goal was not mine alone, and others were supportive whenever they could be. Feeling less isolated was in itself encouraging and relieved some of the stress.

UPON REFLECTION,
here are some takeaways to
Take Care of Your Physical Well-Being:

Performance is not enough for career success.
Focus on your physical well-being, which shines through.
A healthy person is a better performer.

Exercise. Sleep.

Eat right.

Schedule a checkup.

If you work eighteen hours a day, people will expect
eighteen hours a day. Your call.

Dress Matters— Use It as a Strategic Asset

Dress reflects the respect you have for yourself and the respect you have when you interact with others.

Dismiss it as a cliché, but you get no second chance to make a good first impression, and the ambitious employee dresses for a first impression every day. Surely you want that impression to be of someone thoughtfully put together, emanating confidence and showing respect for self and for others. There is no place in that picture for the distraction of cute, sexy, careless or sloppy dressing. Your coworkers have work to do.

An embarrassing experience proved dress to be a strategic asset. Ever since the phrase dress for success became a platitude, we stopped giving it the importance it deserves, which an early lesson about dressing right taught me the hard way. As such lessons go, it shaped my dress behavior for the rest of my life. One day soon after I joined Pfizer in Puerto Rico, I put on the cutest denim outfit for the day. I still think of it as cute. The slacks were snug and the tight vest over a long sleeve white shirt accentuated my girlish figure. And of course, I wore high heels because, at five feet, three inches tall, I always sought to appear taller. I was feeling so pretty as I left for work that morning.

With my morning coffee in hand, I went into my boss's office. He looked up, put on a stern face and said, "What kind of outfit is that to wear to work? You turn around right now, go home and change." I froze, feeling the color drain from my face. Ash white quickly turned to beet red, and when he saw my shock, my boss laughed and said, "I'm just kidding. You look very nice." I walked out of his office quite shaken, because I knew it was no joke. I got the message. Considering how valuable feedback is and how so many leaders mishandle it, that boss tended to mask it with humor. He should have said, "Sylvia, that outfit looks very nice on you, but if you want people to take you seriously, I suggest that you not wear it to work." That might still have been embarrassing, but it would not have shocked me the way his approach did, humorous or not. Although I did not head home, I hid in my office the whole day. The experience served as another defining moment by changing my thinking about how to dress for work. That particular outfit never saw the office again. For many years, slacks were not even a part of my work wardrobe.

Although I would not have chosen to hear feedback the way he said it, my manager did me a favor. I was a young professional—barely thirty and appearing younger—with a high position for my age, so it was important to me to be taken seriously. The lesson came hard but quickly that dress mattered. From then on, my work outfits were dresses, skirts and blouses. Every morning I dressed for work, part of my thinking was whether my attire was appropriate. Sometimes, it is more about the fit and the fabrics than the item. That experience was my introduction to the theme of dressing purposefully for work.

Dressing well does not mean dressing expensively. As a young adult, I was still limited by the economics of my circumstances, but my appearance was always clean and neat—no missing buttons, clothes pressed, shoes shined. These touches require little money, but time and attention which can be controlled regardless of economics.

When you dress well, you feel good about yourself, and as a result you project yourself better. You radiate positive energy, you impart confidence which draws others into experiencing you more positively. Your appearance also communicates the quality of work that can be expected of you: meticulous dress means meticulous work; careless dress means careless work. That is perception.

Over the years, that embarrassing memory came back again and again. As the human resources professional in my unit, I was usually the first person to meet candidates for employment. I toured a full spectrum of dress alternatives from trendy tattered jeans, to stains on a wrinkled shirt, to the eye-catching miniskirt. Their first impressions, their choice of dress for the interview, thus directly colored the decision of whether to present them as candidates to the recruiting manager. When they dressed poorly, they left a bad impression without knowing it. Is that news? When you dress well, you demonstrate respect for yourself and for the people you meet during the day.

Pay Attention to Your Unique Body

In my mid-thirties, I attended a personal development program that included a segment on optimizing personal appearance. At the end of the program, each participant had a private wrap-up session with one of the facilitators. During mine, the facilitator commented that I tended to wear grays and browns and tactfully intimated that those colors made me appear rather…dull. Why had I been wearing so many neutrals? She said I could benefit from a session with a color consultant. With a commitment to do just that, I bought the book *Color Me Beautiful* by Carole Jackson, a popular book at the time. Her new idea was that certain colors bring out the vibrancy of your skin tone and help you convey more energy. Other colors have the opposite effect and drain you of energy visually.

During an eye-opening formal session with a color consultant, I sat in front of a full-length mirror, covered me with a white sheet from my neck down. The consultant then draped fabrics of all the colors of the rainbow across my chest so I could see how my skin reacted to each color. The reds seemed to make my skin pop with brightness, while the browns turned off the lights. Easy diagnosis: Bright Winter. The best colors for me were bright reds, blues and purples—definitely not orange, brown or beige. Green was iffy. The Winter palette tended to brighten my overall skin tone and make me look healthier. The tan-orange-brown spectrum drained the color from my face, so my own wardrobe of browns and tans made me look drab. We discussed the most flattering styles for my height and proportions. Turtleneck sweaters were not flattering because my neck was not long enough. The consultant also cautioned against wearing the wrong size. Some people wear clothes that are too small on them, perhaps out of the vanity of not wanting to admit that they are now a size larger. When the buttons on your outfit are about to pop off or the collar of your favorite shirt starts to dig into your neck, you are overdue to go to the next size. This applies to men and women, though in different ways.

When I got home that day, I made a bee line for my closet and reviewed everything in it. From then on, I worked my wardrobe around my best colors, which also made it easier to mix and match. As I started wearing the brighter colors to work, people complimented me spontaneously about my appearance. The colors made a difference.

Dress Appropriately For Business and Culture

When I returned to New York with Pfizer in 1982, the dress code was fairly easy to figure out, almost like a uniform. Men wore suits, not sport coats. Most women wore suits, some wore dresses. I tended to dress up for work, enjoying looking and feeling special every day I went to work.

In that time of the early 1980's, however, most companies were transitioning to business casual dress. Pfizer resisted the business casual trend for a long time, but in the early 1990's, we finally gave in to the inevitable with a carefully crafted dress policy called 'business appropriate.' The policy, while flexible, reminded employees they were representatives of the company in every work interaction. It asked employees to give some thought to their upcoming day as they considered what to wear. Who would you be meeting with during the day, and what impact did you want to make on those people? What message would your attire send about your company? So if your day included meetings with government officials or colleagues from other companies, more formal attire would be appropriate. If your interactions during the day were less formal, then more casual attire would be acceptable. Of course, there were certain items that were outright taboo: sandals, shorts, jeans, revealing sleeveless tops, collarless shirts.

The business appropriate approach meant that on any given day, employees would be dressed anywhere along the spectrum from crisply casual to full business attire. The beautiful wardrobe I had accumulated did not have to be put aside. If I wanted, I could continue to use my suits and not appear out of place. And when I bought new clothes, I selected styles that allowed the versatility of the casual to formal business look.

Either way, the old habit of checking whether I was appropriately dressed for work became especially important in packing for a trip, and my responsibilities required travel to many countries. How our dress reflects the respect we have for those we meet is particularly important when visiting other cultures. Early in my travels I tended to overpack, to give myself many options once I was there. With experience I was able to pack more lightly yet carefully when preparing for different cultures. For Muslim countries, collared blouses, closed dresses, long sleeves, hems below the knee. For my trips to Pakistan and India, I also bought a couple of shalwar *kameez outfits*—a tunic over wide pants that narrowed at the ankle—which I reserved mostly for business dinners. Local leaders were delighted to see me honor their culture in this way. Whether you are in the U.S. or overseas, you show respect for people by the way you put yourself together, never mimicking, but gently experimenting and balancing it all. At the same time, if a style does not flatter or fit, it will also not help you fit in.

Issues of differing cultures and appropriate dress arose even as I was a little girl growing up in two worlds. As a skinny teenager, I admired the curvy Latinas and dreamed of wearing their low cut, tight fitting dresses. My Mom still smiles at the memory of my favorite dress displayed in a store window on Orchard Street in the Lower East Side of Manhattan—thin straps held up the clingy fabric that wrapped around a shapely figure. I declared that one day I would wear that dress. Well, I never had the figure for that style. Square shouldered and thin, I tended to look better in tailored clothes. I have seen young people at work dressed in a manner more appropriate for the dance floor, pleased that they looked so sexy. Particularly dismaying were the young women who seemed to need the admiring glances to boost their self-esteem.

They were doing themselves a great disservice in terms of the image they created. This is the lesson I learned with my cute denim outfit. It was precisely the cutesiness of it that was inappropriate. If you want to be taken seriously, you need to present yourself as a serious person, clothing included. Anxious to move up, I learned early on that no amount of cute was going to get me there.

Upon reflection, here are some takeaways to Dress Matters:

Be purposeful and meticulous about your dress,
so it works to your advantage.

Being taken seriously starts with doing just that yourself.

Be sensitive to the unique dress culture in your organization
and the changing or unchanging surrounding culture.

Optimize Your Communication Skills

Written and verbal, one-on-one or one-on-many—good communications skills optimize the presentation of self.

Refine Your Skills as a Conversationalist

You walk into the reception, well dressed and exuding the personal energy that comes from being physically fit, in good health and well rested. Soon a senior leader greets you and you're on. Your response will determine whether you sustain the positive and confident appearance you worked so hard to create.

The ability to engage someone in conversation is an important social skill for personal success. The senior leader in the scene appears in receptions, dinners, lobbies and, heaven forbid, elevators. A skillful conversationalist is genuine about her interest in the other person and focuses on things that are important to the other person. When asked

"How are you doing?" she is able to respond in more than monosyllables and in less than a full autobiography.

I had to work long and hard to even come close to being described "skillful conversationalist." It especially made me nervous to strike up a conversation with those in position of authority, so I dreaded work-related receptions and cocktail parties. But I also recognized they were opportunities to become more than a name on paper. I decided to plan for the receptions, fully armed with potential conversation openers. Before attending an event where senior leaders would be present, I did some homework, a little research about the expected attendees, their positions in the organization and whether they had recently made the news. Most leaders were gracious and conscious of their effect on the more junior professionals. Skillful conversationalists themselves, they worked at making us feel comfortable, though it seemed no work at all. Other leaders were more intimidating to approach. In time, I became so comfortable in the reception milieu that colleagues were skeptical when I told them it was hard work for me. Those experiences also taught me that, should leadership come my way, I wanted to be approachable.

Grant Yourself Preparation—Reduce Anxiety

A greater bane, though, was speaking in front of larger audiences than one or two. My discomfort went all the way back to school, where classroom discussions were always stressful, but participation was important to the overall grade. I forced myself to speak up, armed only with clammy hands and a racing heart. What was I afraid of? Only academic suicide. Despite my epiphany in high school about valuing self, I was afraid of making a public fool of myself, afraid of proving to others how stupid I really was. The skill of speaking to a group or an audience eluded me well into my adult years.

As my ninth-grade teacher walked me off the stage following a spectacular fiasco in front of all my classmates, I promised myself that would never happen again. But three years later I faced the possibility that indeed it would happen again. As salutatorian of my high school graduating class, I had to give the welcoming speech at the commencement ceremony. It was a nightmare in the making. I could picture my embarrassment in front of my peers, my teachers and most importantly my family, unless something was done.

To begin with, I worked determinedly on wording of the speech. Many in the audience, like my mother, didn't speak English, only Spanish—I decided to address the audience in both languages. Then, I left nothing else to chance. I sought guidance from my teachers and from my fellow students; I memorized the speech for practicing it out loud; I went to the empty auditorium and rehearsed the entire speech standing on the stage at the podium, to acclimate to the full setting. Incredibly, when the moment came to deliver my speech, I was still nervous and filled with dread. The fight or flight response fully primed, I wanted to flee, but this time I found my voice and, even with a few nervous quivers, delivered my speech to affirming applause.

That was a big moment for me, bigger because I feared repeating the traumatic experience from ninth grade, three years earlier. Instead, I went back to the scene of the crime and erased it. What confidence came with rising to and managing the fear. Complete success would be the day I could stand in front of a large audience without that fear. I had to wait many years for that day to come.

At Barnard College, I was delighted when I saw the class size in my Spanish courses, my major, was six to ten women. The small groups made it easier for me to speak up at least once in every session. I usually met that goal.

However, my minor in education required taking some courses at Teacher's College of Columbia University, where class sizes were much larger. We were required to do practice 'teaches' in front of those large groups. Even though the teaches were barely ten minutes long, they brought me close to hyperventilating before each one. Still in the end, they gave me a little more confidence that I could stand up in front of a group of peers without embarrassing myself. Like readying for the salutatorian speech at high school commencement, the key to a successful presentation was thoroughly successful preparation.

When I taught at the undergraduate level at Queens College, I led a conversational Spanish class—an elective class for advanced students, mostly older than college age. At 23, I stressed over teaching adults in their 30's and 40's. It took me hours deciding what themes we would discuss and how to stimulate the conversation. The hours of preparation ultimately produced a half page that teased up the theme for a 90-minute guided conversation. It was nerve-wracking but mostly self induced, because I knew more Spanish than the students and so could effectively address any questions posed. Yet, the fear of embarrassing myself was still there.

In the business world, presentations to senior leaders were a regular part of the annual business cycle, and once again I experienced some anxiety and invested long hours into preparation. I would show up with binders of back-up data in addition to multiple reminder notes on my slides. My nervous energy manifested itself by rushing the presentations. Any silent moments seemed like an eternity, but I dutifully filled the empty air with 'um's. In a presentation skills seminar, we joked that most people would rather die than speak in public and risk both professional suicide and death by humiliation. Sometimes I felt that way.

Two years in the training group developed my presentation skills, but the stress level was compounded by subjects less familiar than Spanish or Human Resources. My colleagues appeared to walk into the room with nothing but the course materials, confident in their core expertise. They seemed to have a bottomless collection of stories and examples to illustrate their points. I, on the other hand, walked into the room with the course book fully annotated along the margins and decorated with multicolor Post-It notes to remind me of indispensable points. My preparation was intense, practicing out loud—because my voice sounds different out loud than in my head—always checking out the meeting space beforehand and becoming familiar with the necessary audiovisual equipment. If it was a speech, I stood at the stage podium and rehearsed the text out loud. I did everything I could to take charge of the situation, to be as familiar as possible with the surroundings. In spite of the stress that was a constant shadow, the effort paid off with success at presenting a poised and confident exterior. Most people did not realize the level of my inner discomfort.

Plan Your Actions and Starve Your Fear

As my responsibilities grew, the ability to address large groups became a critical skill for success. I was able to present well and appear relaxed, but internally my stress levels were high. The preparation allowed me to speak competently, but because I could never fully relax, how could I be at my best? The anxiety was a constant each and every time. A glutton for punishment, I would actively volunteer to speak, hoping the increased experience would increase the comfort level. By putting myself in those situations and working through the fear, I gained a little more confidence with each experience—though painfully slow. Each time brought a little less panic as I was learning to trust the knowledge inside me. My reputation as a speaker, in turn, drew more invitations to present to large audiences.

The road to success was not without its potholes. Once I was asked to speak at an orientation program to 285 new employees from throughout the U.S. It was a last-minute request, but I agreed in spite of feeling less prepared than usual. Not my best performance, I cringed as I reviewed the evaluation forms afterwards. So many participants mentioned "tedious ums" to bother me enough to get back on the horse and volunteer for the next orientation session three months later. This time, I had plenty of time to prepare. I also asked a friend to sit in on my presentation and watch out for ums, speaking too fast or whatever else detracted from my presentation. She was one of the best public speakers I knew, and I trusted that she would not be shy about giving feedback. After the 90-minute program, I was relieved to hear there were only three ums in all, the evaluations were very positive and there were no comments about tedious ums. I learned my lesson again— preparation—and I could move on.

Trust Your Own Knowledge

How deeply rooted was my fear of public speaking? While confidence in my knowledge laid the foundation for success, anxiety spread out like a mental block between me and that knowledge. Reminding myself, whether I was presenting to senior management or to a class, who was the most knowledgeable person in the room about the subject connected me to my confidence.

A culminating moment of confidence came in Washington D.C. as the keynote speaker at a Pfizer-sponsored conference of nearly 2,000 small business leaders. Earlier that day, I had practiced my speech on stage. I felt prepared and relaxed. Waiting for my slot second in the program, I noticed the first speaker was getting no attention, with everyone in the audience talking at their tables. Boredom? Rudeness? The noise was such that even sitting on stage, I had trouble hearing the speaker, and then I was introduced. How could I earn their attention and interest? It would have been a real farce to deliver a speech to so many leaders who had shut down their attention. Instead, I joined them: "There's a great buzz in this room, a reflection of the tremendous energy here today, and that's good! Now I have something important to say that you will want to hear. If I could have your attention, you won't be disappointed." The buzz died down, and my delivery ended to tremendous applause. My colleagues were astounded how 'masterfully' I had gotten the audience's attention. I relish the memory of that moment—no anxiety, no stress, no ignoring the elephant in the room. I had arrived at a place where I could think effectively about what to do to make myself heard. It had taken me a long time to get there.

Keep Your Dialogue Standards High Even in Writing

The importance of verbal communications, both conversational and public speaking, has been my focus because of its key in presentation of self and because of my own biggest challenges. In tandem with speaking well, good writing is also important to presentation of self—a base skill that should be solid graduating high school and mastered when you graduate college. Nonetheless, many well-educated people write poorly, and while some math or science geniuses can get away with it, it reflects poorly back onto the individual. In today's world of email communications, a lot of dialogue takes place in the written word, making writing skills even more important. The most recent texting craze can cause a decrease in writing skills because our young people get used to abbreviations and short-cuts. Have fun learning the new abbreviations, but make sure you are also able to compose full sentences, paragraphs, memos, announcements and reports. Written dialogues also present you to others and create perceptions of who you are—lasting impressions.

UPON REFLECTION,
here are some takeaways to
Optimize Your Communication Skills:

Good speech and writing are critical to optimal presentation of self.

Take great care in the written word.
Speech has nuance; writing lasts longer.

Preparation overcomes the fear of public speaking.

Part Seven

Working Woman, Working Mother

Success in a Man's World

When you walk into a room, you walk in with your gender, your ethnicity and every other characteristic that distinguishes you from the group.

Being a girl never seemed like a barrier to my dreams. Only ethnicity and poverty overwhelmed me by gnawing at my self-esteem. The subject of gender was a minor issue in my experience from childhood to early adulthood. Puerto Rican, poor, but blind to gender issues. Yes, it was unfair that my brothers were altar boys at our church, and as girls, my sisters and I were excluded. Then at home, the boys had more freedom and could go out to play unsupervised, while we could not. Yet these disparities appeared to be due to our church and Latin culture.

Not one school experience, positive or negative, laid itself at the door of gender. Girls achieved academic excellence the same as boys. Men and women taught school. Barnard, a women's college, reinforced gender pride. Many women were professors in my field of study as well as in my chosen career, education. A very competent woman was my first department head at the start of my teaching high school.

Deal with the Burden of Being First and only

In the shift from education to the business world, though, ethnicity receded into the background while my gender jumped in front and center. Of course, moving back to Puerto Rico, I was no minority. However, my experiences were odd for being the only woman then on the leadership team and the first woman to ever reach that level. Many of the women who worked on the production lines and in clerical and professional positions were proud that a woman was on the leadership team. There would be no disappointing them. My success or failure could reflect on all women. My superiors and peers, everyone male, encouraged and supported me during those early days in business, demonstrating genuine interest in my success. I worked hard to live up to their expectations.

Throughout my career, being the only woman in many of my work groups, often the first woman to hold the position was a non-event. Until very late in my career, my bosses were male, good bosses for the most part who treated me fairly, pushed me to excel and sponsored me right up the career ladder.

Don't Assume it's Always Discrimination

Nevertheless, during my thirty years in the corporate world, there were many situations that could be attributed to gender discrimination, in the heat of the moment. In retrospect, it was less clear. Anyone could conclude a more likely factor was my youth at play; other times, it was definitely gender.

The lessons of self-reliance and confidence learned as a young minority in New York City were a source of strength in these new circumstances. They engendered a strong affirmation of self—my sense of worth depended on me, on my own understanding of my capabilities. It was inner directed and not reliant on the approval of others. No one would make me the victim of ignorance or bigotry without my support, and there would be none of that. Driven to succeed and ambitious, I strove to grow professionally within the realities of a business environment. But achievement in a corporate environment would not be as straightforward as in school where I succeeded by performing through sheer force, measured in grades. No, performance is not enough. Other dynamics affect our ability to reach higher levels in an organization, specifically, how we display and portray ourselves to others: presentation of self.

The universal reality was that my gender walked into every meeting with me, maybe ahead of me. As a result, my experiences differed from those of men, though the same can be said about you as an individual if you diverge from the norm of the group. Height, weight, ethnicity, age, outspokenness, even a handsome face and other characteristics that set you apart are all dynamics contributing to how a group sees you. Usually, try as I might to fit in, I was shorter and younger than most, the single Hispanic or minority, and always female. Many times, it was unclear whether an unpleasant experience was due to any single attribute. My growing habit was to consider other dynamics that might have been at play, or if I could have acted differently. Unless there was considerable proof of gender bias, I resisted blaming anatomy.

When I transferred to the Corporate Training and Development

Group, my first assignment put me in San Diego, California, teaching a very rigorous, week-long program I had taught many times, but in Spanish. San Diego would be the first time teaching the program in English, and the stress threatened to resurrect the old feelings of insecurity. The stars were aligned against me that week, as the all-male group was comprised of seasoned managers, many there for a getaway. The classroom, on the ground level of a hotel, had wall-to-wall windows facing the pool and sheer curtains barely blocking the bikini view. In the evening, most of the class went to the local clubs and showed up in the morning suffering from the effects of too much alcohol and too little sleep. Since most of them did not want to be in the classroom, they challenged everything I said. I prepped and reviewed the next day's material late into the night, and when they tested me further, I struggled to remain true to the program. Foolish me—young and focused on the job at hand. Wisecracking class—older and out to have a good time. The end of the week came as a great relief. Back at the office, my manager told me that the senior member of the class had complained about my 'inflexibility.' Let down, I described what had happened and then tried not to squirm as my manager coached me about customizing programs to the "Personality of the group." Which personality was that? A twelve-year-old's? It almost felt like adding insult to injury.

As a representative of the corporate group, I needed to develop skills to handle such groups. Yet, I was certain that the group would not have been as rebellious had the instructor been male. With the passage of time, the program still looks like it was a failure, lacking a skillful approach of addressing the group dynamics. On the other hand, there is no excuse for rude behavior. Gender was an ugly factor, but grace and experience could have triumphed.

One frustrating experience and I was introduced to business training in the U.S., but determined to do better next time. Next time turned out to be just a few months later, when Pfizer sent me as a last minute substitute for back-to-back programs in Sandwich, England where we had a Research & Development center. This time I focused on understanding the groups before I arrived in England—all scientists and again all male. Because they were excited about Edward de Bono's work on creative thinking, they worried that the rational process I was teaching would stifle creativity. So on the long flight across the Atlantic, de Bono's book was my bible until I was conversant about creative thinking and able to weave the concepts into the rational process curriculum. The program participants first appreciated that I had taken the time to understand de Bono's work, then conceded they could incorporate some aspects of rational process without stifling innovation. They did challenge the program, but in a professional way, which left me flying home more confident about managing the program.

Two positive experiences back-to-back now counterbalanced San Diego. A more balanced perspective on the San Diego revealed that, gender dynamics aside, my preparation and my own training had been wanting in the face of taking on such a difficult group. It would not be the only time to experience such resistance. Wisdom showed it pays to customize whatever the material to fit the group, and with experience I also felt confident enough to modify the core design of the programs for better effectiveness.

One experience where gender was clearly an issue occurred during a career move into another part of the Company. In a conversation about my aspirations, one of the senior leaders endorsed my goals, but confided that it was unlikely to happen because the current man in charge of the group did not think it was any place for a woman. The leader was courageous for being so candid, but I was stunned. Having worked so hard to overcome discrimination on the basis of my ethnicity, I now had to deal with bias on the basis of my body, terribly discouraging. Thinking I could never get into that group, I naïvely questioned the overall integrity of the company. We had a clear-cut policy against discrimination: "Don't do it." Yet here it was staring me in the face, a black & white reality check regarding how far my career could grow. However, that courageous leader also asked me to be patient instead of frustrating myself uselessly, "You are young and have plenty of time to grow your career. With the other leader nearing retirement, a more enlightened leader would take his place."

And so it was. A lot changed within a year and who else ended up heading the group but my candid coach—I was one of his early appointments. This experience gave me a dose of reality, never forgetting that while a man temporarily blocked my career due to nonsense, it was also a man who sponsored me to the next rung.

Another experience taught me how easy it is to get it all wrong. I applied for a position in a division of the company where women were also very scarce. Throughout a very positive set of interviews, I was optimistic of being selected. Then I got the phone call: someone else, a man, was chosen. At that time, it was obvious I missed the job just because I was a woman. Without proof, I let it go. Many years later, I ran into the leader who made that decision, and he explained that a restructuring in another area had displaced a qualified man. The leader had been asked to place that man in the open position. If management had only told me back then, I could certainly have understood the situation. We have to be careful with assumptions. For many years, I had assumed myself to be the victim of gender discrimination in a case that was simply a business decision—not a better choice, but not a biased one either.

One experience concerning independence crystallized the ethnic and gender issues like no other. Conversation at dinner with a number of colleagues came around to a mention that my parents lived with me. A respected colleague turned to me with a surprised look and said, "I thought you were an independent woman!" The comment was plainly judgmental and, especially from this colleague, floored me. My parents had been my life preserver much of my adult life, and with increasing financial security, the roles slowly reversed. I was very happy to be the one to provide a comfortable home and financial support all around. In the Hispanic community, parents and grandparents are an integral part of their children's lives, so it is quite typical and expected that parents live with them when grown, too. Financial support, if necessary, is also the norm. In addition, I had worked very hard for my independence, to rely on no one financially, to send my son to college without loans, to travel the world on my own and to depend solely on myself to get out of tight situations. My colleague's careless attack questioned all of that. Without snapping at him, I simply looked him straight in the eye and said with a smile, "I am." Awkwardly, he got the message and changed the subject.

Contend with the Day-to-Day Reminders, Don't Sweat the Small Stuff

Daily life brought frequent reminders that I was a woman in a big world I did not control. One day a male colleague and I were standing in front of his office when a client of his in upper management stopped by. The senior manager greeted my colleague and handed me a stack of documents to copy for him. Stunned, but recovering quickly and poker-faced, I said "I would be glad to help, but I don't know how to operate the copier." It took the manager barely a second to realize his faux pas, as he turned beet red and uttered a flustered apology. He had assumed, for only one reason, that the person standing next to his male contact must be the administrative assistant. His behavior was rather stupid— this was the 1980's, not the 1950's—but hardly malicious. Minor exchanges such as those signaled I was an intruder in this world. Good, kind men committed such slip-ups regularly, clumsy at dealing with women in more senior positions. And while I could understand 'no malice intended,' those frequent reminders always retained their annoyance factor.

My responsibilities often required overseas travel. Due to the long and tiring flights, my seat was often booked in Business or First Class with very few other women. The flight attendants were noticeably less attentive to me than to the men. Maybe someone was being oversensitive, perhaps imaginative. Yet the consistent behavior had to be accepted for what it was—gender discrimination, this time by women, since most attendants on those flights were women. The problem was not men, but accepted social norms. These observations puzzled my male colleagues who also travelled a lot. On one trip with a man who had initially pooh-poohed my take as overly sensitive about gender, he sat on the aisle seat and I took the window. As the plane leveled off into cruising altitude, the flight attendant asked my colleague if he was comfortable. Did he need a pillow? Did he get his menu? Did he have any questions about the menu? He smiled happily that he was fine, thank you, and she walked on to the next row. The chance to prove what I had been saying fell into my lap, "Did you see that? Am I invisible?" He just guffawed, realizing he had been oblivious to it until I pointed it out. When he saw it for himself, he fully absorbed that it was not oversensitivity, it was right there. He called the flight attendant and said "My colleague would also like a menu." Called back, she got the point without another word. What a relief that someone who did not experience my life as I experienced it also saw my point. Regardless of whether the flight attendant purposely meant to discriminate, the behavior was discriminatory. The tall, male executive was the more important person in her mind. These mindless, thoughtless behaviors can diminish you if you allow them to.

In the course of a typical workday, sports conversations often prevailed: the weekend golf game, football or baseball. Last night's game was typical pre-meeting or coffee station talk. Those exchanges would segue into stories about past military experiences, and while I could hold my own with baseball, I was just a bystander with other sports, boot camp or combat. Since informal conversations could not be expected to limit themselves to my personal knowledge base, my choices seemed to be: either suffer through the conversation or leave the room unnoticed. With more experience and confidence, though, it was easy enough to say, "I'm sorry that I can't contribute much to this conversation." Most of the time, men would get the hint and politely move on to more universal ground. Not wanting to be the one to stifle their commonality every time I was in the room, and since some women were conversant in sports, I tried to become more informed of the basics. Sometimes my son would call me early morning to tell me about the big sport event of the weekend or the upcoming Monday night game, to keep me from being totally ignorant.

Those same colleagues would get together after work or on weekends for a game of golf or tennis. The informal encounters then sometimes led to business conversations to be continued later or introductions to contacts that could have a positive influence on their careers because of the social connection. An advantage that junior male employees have is using the same bathroom as senior executives. The one informal venue I had was the fitness center. Many of the men attended the company gym and because we were in the same activity with a common goal, good health, a sense of camaraderie developed there. One day I was huffing and puffing on the exercise bike, when the president of our division walked by. One look at my sweaty, red face and he blurted out, "You look like shit!" We both laughed, and I exclaimed, "Hopefully, it's temporary." For me, the key was recognizing his 'guy talk' as a playful compliment, which made me more relaxed around him after that exchange.

Although rare, a few awkward situations brought unsolicited male attention. Early in my career, I was traveling with a senior leader who became overly friendly with me. Ever so politely, I asked if he thought it was appropriate behavior. He stepped back and made a joke to bridge the awkward moment—it never happened again. But I wondered whether my career had just gone down the tubes. He was a senior leader in a position to influence my career positively or negatively. Luckily, with good sense and diplomacy, our friendship remained intact. He became my sponsor, and a few years later his recommendation helped me get a promotion to Director.

Choose Wisely How You Respond—Do Not Escalate

Rudeness, bias or impropriety, the trick in handling sticky situations that cross the line is in responding firmly without making things worse. Often the first or only woman in my position, I would have nothing of crying to daddy by reporting personal problems from my trips. Awkward situations called for clever dealings that did not make matters worse. If my response was to cause a big scene, people would remember the scene and bury the improper behavior that triggered my response. "Boy, she really has a short fuse!" they could conclude, or "She doesn't know how to handle delicate situations." Plus, the multiple dynamics at play—gender, ethnicity, youth, size, height, nationality—made the situations experienced as negative hard to pin on one attribute alone.

Most important to me was protecting my sense of worth, not to allow another person's out-of-place behavior to erode who I was. Not my core, not my composure. The lessons of the defining moments of my youth still held: you will not experience erosion of self, your value as a human being, unless you allow it. When you retain a strong sense of self, your emotions do not control you, either, thereby freeing you to formulate an objective and appropriate response of your choice. Anger tends to ambush good efforts, because the angrier you become, the less in control you are of your actions. If you can force me to agree with you, you control me. Yet if you can force me into an automatic reaction, you control me still. It helps to remind yourself that no one can force you to act in any particular way—you are free to respond as you want. The best response to an ugly situation is one that builds rather than destroys: demonstrate to the individual, brilliantly, that a particular behavior is inappropriate without ever attacking the individual. In many situations, an individual clearly hurt by offensive behavior lashes back in anger and attacks. Such behavior invites the offender to say "See what I mean?" That victim may then win the immediate battle of wits and lose the war. But battles matter less than the big win.

In situations where someone broadcasts negative intent, it helps to keep an open mind. Before you decide, flip things around and consider what else the person might have meant. Just thinking it through that way tends to diffuse the internal reaction and allow you to respond in a constructive way. This is not to advocate that you avoid the issue when you are the target of obvious discriminatory behavior. No, it is not okay to just let that go, but take great care not to reinforce the stereotype the offender is using to judge you.

In the field of Human Resources, I often had to sift through supervisor-employee conflicts to listen objectively and reach a fair solution. First, I had to listen to both sides of each story. Indeed, there were always two sides that told two different viewpoints to the same story. Too many people attribute negative intent to the behavior of others and then respond based only on that assumption. Things go downhill from there. For example, you get angry you were not invited to an important meeting. You just know it was intentional, then you sulk, lose trust in the other person and even look for ways to get even. What if the person who sent the invitation simply missed adding you, or was unaware that you belong on the invitation list? A simple call to clarify will prevent the long-term impact of your resentment.

Don't Expect Success in a Man's World without Male Mentors

My goal is to demonstrate objectivity and balance in my narrative. There is no time to waste getting even with people who put up obstacles. The fact is I did make it to the top—the second woman to hold the highest Human Resources position in over 155 years of history at Pfizer and the very first to do it from the inside. Regardless of the many challenges along the way, as a woman in this big world, no one could have made it to the top without the mentoring and sponsorship of the men who had the power in that very world. My gratefulness matched their great position of power. Men took big chances on me, promoting me to big jobs at a very young age—sometimes with fingers crossed, but believing I could do it. Men appointed me to jobs that no woman had before. Men held me to the same standards they held male colleagues. Men gave me tough feedback, painful too, trusted me with confidential information that if misused, could have harmed their own careers. Nothing to sneeze at.

And Yet, Look at the Statistics...

It took twenty five years for me to meet my first female boss. She demonstrated a selflessness and courage that surpassed many of my previous bosses. I reveled in the freedom to be myself, a woman, a mother, and a daughter. I would have benefited from that kind of relationship as a young professional.

The facts about women in the workplace are too frustrating. Raw statistics show that women lag badly in most categories when compared to men. One study comes from Catalyst, a non-profit research group that works with businesses to help create an inclusive environment and expand opportunities for women. According to Catalyst, in 2009 women held only 13.5% of executive officer positions in Fortune 500 companies, and women on corporate boards hover similarly at the 15% level. Even this picture is much improved from twenty five years before that. Women are making headway in every profession, although there is a long stretch to travel to reach equality.

While outright, purposeful discrimination is rare these days, many practices, often difficult to identify, have harmed certain groups within an organization. An analogy from grammar school science on osmosis serves here. If you put salt in a bucket of water, the salt content in the water soon stabilizes throughout. Only a physical barrier can prevent all the water from having the same salinity level. Similarly, when the composition of a workforce does not reflect the same composition as its source of employees—whether a community, the state, a region or the country—some barrier must exist that gets in the way of absorption as natural as osmosis. Proactive organizations continually analyze their workforces for these discrepancies and work to correct them. When you consider barriers, you must think about our society, with the messages that we give our children at home and at school, and the barriers that we are creating along the way. During my thirty years in business, I saw the benefits of all of this good work. When I retired, there were many more women in positions of leadership than when I began. There has been considerable improvement, and it will continue to improve.

Look Forward to our Grandchildren's World

My husband and I go on a rigorous wilderness trip every year where we canoe, hike and camp out. We have made this trip for seventeen years now, and in our early trips we would run into other groups, mostly men on fishing trips. But over the years, the makeup of these other groups has changed significantly. We still run into the all-male fishing parties, but now we also run into groups of young men and women enjoying the great outdoors. And it is amazing to see strong, young women flip the canoes over their heads and carry them across the trail to the next lake. It seems natural to both genders: whoever has the turn to carry the canoe, carries it. Period.

This is the world of my grandchildren, growing up where neither gender nor ethnicity nor any other type of distinguishing characteristic form absolute barriers to their dreams. During my 'growing up' in the corporate world, often the only woman in a work team, the dynamics of flying solo was all mine to handle. But later in my career and certainly by the time of retirement, it was very rare to see a work team that did not include more than one woman. There has been so much progress in the last twenty years that it would be unnatural for the momentum to come to a sudden stop. May this perception be more than my tendency to look at things positively. Logically, denying any segment of our population the right to participate in the economic health of the world is not good business. Discrimination denies us the energy, the thinking, the creativity that all humanity can bring to our society. Every time we have a first—the first Catholic President, the first black president, the first woman President—it is a milestone in our history. The next time a black man runs for President won't be as dramatic.

Naturally, there is little greater joy than watching my grandchildren at play. My granddaughter enjoys her dolls, and my grandson enjoys his laser guns. They do not really play with each other when engaged in those games, but they both enjoy electronic games and compete fiercely in this common interest. I like to think of this as an analogy to the world they will enjoy as adults. They will both be able to enjoy activities and roles defined by gender even as they both reach for the stars.

UPON REFLECTION,
here are some takeaways to
Succeed in a Man's World:

When you face awkward situations, stand up for yourself
in a way that burns no bridges.

Do not waste time attributing negative intent to other people's
behavior and then responding based only on that assumption,
a fancy word for guessing.

Do not allow the thoughtless behaviors of others to diminish you.

A Single Working Mother

To cope with the ever-present guilt of a single working mother, preserve a sense of your personal dignity and accomplishment.

Coping as a Single Mother, Guilty as Charged

One of the reasons for procrastinating on getting a divorce was my concern over the impact on my son, Kenny. Why not just cope for his sake? How self-centered can you be? Even though he was aware of the conflict between his parents, my son was a happy little boy. *Abuelita* and *Abuelito* had cared for him since birth, the same as for my sister's son Ruben, so Kenny had a playmate who was more like a brother. The few hours that Kenny spent at home with me were further diluted by my schoolwork, and with my husband often getting home late, our family time was limited.

Kenny handled the divorce well, mainly because he still had *Abuelita* and *Abuelito*. But that changed a few months later when my parents moved to Puerto Rico. They spent all their savings and more to buy a house back 'home.' Since we had planned to live with them until we could purchase our own house, the announcement of our divorce exploded like a land mine in Eden. Needing first to establish my independence, I announced my plan to remain in New York and move in temporarily with my sister Miriam. My parents had no choice but to carry out their plans and depart, heartbroken, for Puerto Rico.

There was really no way to predict how Kenny would react when he lost his grandparents in this fashion. My happy little boy soon became insecure and frightened of things that had never scared him. I did not fare much better myself. Earlier that year, my regular teaching job ended, and the divorce took the last four hundred dollars I had. Every week my position as substitute teacher changed to a different school, which kept renewing my experience of how tough kids can be when their regular teachers are out. But more upsetting was not being able to figure out a satisfactory childcare arrangement for once-happy Kenny. My need to show that I could do it all alone paled in comparison to my worry for him. Later that summer, I wrote to my parents and they responded immediately with one-way tickets to Puerto Rico.

We quickly got back to a familiar routine: I taught school, now at the university level, and Kenny started school in first grade. *Abuelita* and *Abuelito* cheerfully resumed their roles as his primary caregivers. But Kenny knew that our family unit was not exactly right. He reasoned that a family is not complete without a mommy and *a daddy*, figuring he could do something about it. It became his mission to find me a new husband. Soon after the divorce, at an event with family and friends, he overheard that one of the guests was single, male and adult. Perfect. At the top of his voice, he hawked his merchandise, "My mommy is single too, and she's looking to get married!" As my jaw dropped and both cheeks turned red, everyone else roared with laughter. On another occasion, a man invited us to a picnic. As we took off, Kenny blurted out from the back seat, "So, are you going to marry my mom?" As I tried to disappear into my own seat, my unruffled friend calmly said, "Well, young man, we'll have to think about that." As humorous as these episodes were, that is how much they broke my heart for expressing a child's call and underlying need for a traditional family.

After joining the pharmaceutical industry, I was able to enroll my eight-year-old in the local Catholic school. Two years later, stepping up to Pfizer, I had to relocate to another town nearer to work and moved Kenny with me. My parents would have kept him, but it was important to me that he knew he could always count on me, never to feel that he was a burden. Again he attended the local Catholic school, with after-school care from a teacher friend who was also able to tutor him. He was not thrilled with this arrangement and made a case the next year for "No babysitter. I am eleven. I can walk straight home from school and do my own homework until you get home from work." To make sure that he got home safely, I would call every day after school. It was a shame that my decisions were creating the settings that potentially put him in danger.

Meanwhile, my parents returned to New York. They had been devastated when I moved for work and stole their grandson away. Although we were spending almost every weekend with them, they were lonely for him. These two wonderful people, who had dedicated their entire married lives to their children and then grandchildren, were not happy living alone. So they packed up and went to live with my sister Elba in New York. There, in spite of the cramped situation, they felt useful caring for her two children and allowing her to work. From then on, my son spent every school break in New York with his grandparents and his sibling cousins. During the school year, he was in

Puerto Rico, but the latchkey arrangement was no fun for him, so it was no surprise when he asked if he could stay in New York fulltime. My feelings for him were deep. If I let him live in New York, we might lose the close relationship we had. There I was, responsible and guilty for creating this dilemma and causing more stress in his life. I said no, and he accepted it with disappointment.

That summer, an unexpected opportunity came my way to work in Pfizer New York, and no need to think twice about it. I would move back to New York, and even though my new job meant frequent travel, Kenny would be in a stable home environment with his grandparents. All three were ecstatic when I told them that their prayers had been answered.

Having made that decision, I then thought about my son's transition. Remembering my own transition as a little girl, I was adamant that my son be placed in the appropriate grade, sixth grade. Fortunately, his frequent trips to New York and my insistence on speaking English with him had kept him fairly strong conversationally, though he would have to take placement exams. We were not worried about his demonstrating grade level Math, but he really needed to improve on formal English grammar. To that end, my sister-in-law, Pearl, tutored him over the summer. Ken remembers how difficult it was to learn "All the rules and then the exceptions, and exceptions to the exceptions." Nonetheless, success, he was placed in sixth grade, and although the first six months were tough, soon he was just another sixth grader.

Decide for Yourself—No One to Share the Consequences

One unanticipated stress of single parenthood was not having an equal partner to share decisions about *our* son. The buck stopped with me, no one else to share the blame if something went wrong. Even though my parents remained reliable and supportive, I was the one making the decisions for Kenny. It worried me what he was missing by not having a father in his day-to-day life. I was not lonely for myself. My father was a wonderful role model, but when questions arose where I would have said, "Go ask your father," it did not feel right saying, "Go ask your grandfather." Remembering my commitment "You can always count on me," I tried to fill that role myself. When I did not feel up to going to the beach and Kenny insisted on knowing why, it was time to talk about a woman's cycle. When he wanted more about the birds and the bees, we read a book together. My ears always perked up when conversations veered toward the impact of single motherhood on children.

Nonetheless, it was a great relief to be able to travel without displacing my son. He remained at home, doted on by his grandparents, and his normal routine continued uninterrupted. I was often away for a month at a time, calling home regularly and sending postcards—we did that in those days—from the cities I visited. I also took him on vacation to Spain and Italy to understand more about my job. But my frequent and extensive travels remained a deep source of guilt.

Keep the Career Focus and Don't Beat Yourself Up

Had I not been acutely focused on my career, who would do that for me? I observed how successful people, mostly men, behaved at work. It seemed that frequent travel, dining out and long hours were the norm for them. Anyone with career ambitions accepted and even enjoyed the pace, as did I. Most of them were fortunate to have spouses at home with the kids. And since I was competing with the best, I too travelled extensively, dined out and consistently worked long hours. Avoiding positions requiring such travel, I could have worked eight-hour days, five-day weeks, but I was ambitious and felt I had to work harder to compete. Besides, I loved my work, the learning, the challenge, the travel. Unwilling to pass on any of it, I lived with the guilt.

My parents were at home, gladly dedicated to their grandchildren. As more women joined the corporate race, I could appreciate my blessings. Many of them were mothers without built-in sitters, struggling to be good both as mothers and as executives. Some could afford nannies. Others tried working part-time. Many pulled out of the race, and the rest stoically stood their ground and worked through complications. Whatever the details, we all seemed to deal with a level of remorse for what damage we might be doing either to our kids or to our careers. Or both.

The women who seemed to deal best with the duality of motherhood and career had the most powerful inner sense of self, personal dignity and pride in their accomplishments. So once again, my mantra. When you value who and what you are, you can face the most extraordinary challenges that life throws at you.

Additionally, children are more resilient than they get credit for. I second-guessed myself endlessly when it came to my son, but as an adult with his own family, he tells a different tale. While he may have wished for an intact family unit and a real sibling, a lot of the issues that bothered me did not loom as large for him. He says, "It's like when kids fall down; they bounce up because it's harder to break their bones. I tended to get over things much faster than Mom who always shed a harsher light on the situation." He is right. I was judging myself all the time and coming up short.

How did all this affect my son? He learned the importance of a well-chosen marriage and making sure that the woman would be the woman with whom he could live the rest of his life. Setting the bar so high, I inadvertently created stress for my future daughter-in-law who, after five years of dating, wanted to know "What his intentions were." And when. They married and have worked very hard to provide an intact family for their two children. After much agonizing when their second child was born, my daughter-in-law decided to stay home. My son does not have the need or the desire to climb the career ladder his mother climbed. He avoids jobs that require frequent travel and works from home when possible. They are thoroughly involved in their children's activities, and they make sure the grandparents, and great-grandparents, too, are an important part of their children's lives. My son's deep commitment to his immediate and extended family is a result of his experience growing up in a one-parent home and of his deep love of his grandparents. Ken tells me that he believed, even as a little boy, that I always did what would be best for him in the long run. He appreciates that he and his family are beneficiaries of the sacrifices I made, thus giving him choices I did not have.

In the course of my thirty-year career, I experienced the business world's growing support for the women in their workforce. The competition for talent makes it just good business, no more or less, to offer subsidized child care arrangements, more generous maternity benefits and a work environment that understands the special issues of this segment of the workforce. As social norms changed, the stigma associated with single motherhood also faded to the point where more women are single mothers by choice. Nonetheless, as my daughter-in-law demonstrated during her personal debate to stay home or return to work after the birth of her second child, it will never be an easy decision. Women will always be balancing the pros and cons of being a stay-home mom, working outside in a career, or both. Whatever the choice, personal happiness depends on maintaining a core sense of personal value and accomplishment so necessary to every human being.

UPON REFLECTION,
here are some takeaways to
A Single Working Mother:

Relax. Children are more resilient than you think.

Give your children the certainty that they are loved.

Maintain a personal sense of value and accomplishment.

Part Eight

Leadership

Leadership

The skills that you need to lead people effectively are the same whether you're a supervisor on a packaging line of a manufacturing facility or the president of a multi-million dollar business.

My first exposure to people in charge was the foreman of the sugar cane plantation where my father worked in rural Puerto Rico. My parents both spoke of him with respect, affection and a certain sense of awe. My father experienced many bosses over the years, and he always spoke of them with respect, but sometimes there was a slight element of fear. Those early memories followed me throughout my life as a leader. Because I tended to see my father within those who held the most humble positions on the job, I went out of my way to get to know them and to treat them with respect. As a leader, I wanted to be approachable, never feared.

When I first became a supervisor, I was untrained and

inexperienced in leadership, which did not come automatically. However, my role in Human Resources gave me a unique perspective on good and bad leaders: many personnel issues involved conflicts between subordinate and supervisor. The best managers had an innate respect for people. They were good at guiding and giving feedback. They made sure their people knew what to do and had the resources they needed to get it done. These experiences showed me a lot about what to do and what not to do, but as a neophyte supervisor, I was still making my share of mistakes, and incompetence filled the remaining vacuum.

Help Others Perform and Succeed

A pivotal transition in a manager's career is the move from individual contributor to supervisor, a paradigm shift that many have difficulty making successfully. For one thing, they go from being evaluated on their own work to being evaluated on the work of their group.

Take a salesperson who depends on her individual efforts to exceed her sales targets. She dedicates a lot of time to the things that develop a sales territory, such as providing exceptional customer service and attracting new customers. One day the company acknowledges her success in sales by promoting her to sales manager. Similarly, a successful teacher is assigned as principal of his school. The moment the salesperson and the teacher are promoted to manager and principal, respectively, their jobs change. Now they must use their success to make sure the people who report to them are successful. Leaders have to use their knowledge and expertise to help each subordinate become as good as or better than the leader had been in that position. This is a major change—and success in this new role requires different skills.

It was this transition of perspectives that gave me the most trouble as a novice supervisor. With pride in my own reputation for dependability and quality work, I continued to work in the same way that was successful for me in the past. The work of my direct reports was as familiar to me as if it was my handiwork. I scrutinized the work coming out of my department to ensure that reports were accurate, and I set up elaborate follow-up systems to make certain deadlines were met. If one of my people made a mistake, it felt like my mistake. Before long, feedback said I spent too much time looking over their shoulders. I had forgotten how it felt when my bosses micromanaged me, as when one personally reviewed my math in a compensation proposal and demonstrated he did not trust me. There I was, giving the same message to my staff, because I did not trust them to do the work as well as I could have. The most important responsibility of being a successful supervisor had slipped my mind—to help my people be successful.

One of my bosses was a great role model in consistently applying and actually modeling what I call Management 101: Tell them what is expected of them, give them feedback, and make sure they have what they need to do the job. Early each year, we would agree on my objectives—*tell them what is expected of them*. Every three months, we would review my progress—*give them feedback*. Then we discussed what obstacles I was facing or what I needed further to accomplish my objectives—*make sure they have what they need to do the job*. At the end of the year, the cycle culminated in a performance discussion. That boss never skimped on the performance process. His dedication could be trusted, because no matter how busy we were during the year, I would have my periodic air time. At that time, he would be focused on me and thoughtful in his comments, while he otherwise gave me a lot of freedom to succeed or fail. Either way, I could count on him to be there to acknowledge the success or help me through the problems.

Some leaders thought all of that 'stuff' was unnecessary at senior levels. Very early in my career, I was thrilled to be assigned to a high-ranking leader as his Human Resources representative, because he was the most senior leader I had worked for up to that point. He was a very astute businessman, but he did not interact a lot with his people. When one of his newly appointed vice presidents inquired how work performance would be measured, I decided to speak to the senior leader about setting objectives and having regular discussions with his people. It was hard to get an appointment with him, but I finally walked into his huge office, where he was sitting behind a massive desk, looking very serious and impatient. I quickly came to the point about the value of objectives, feedback and guidance. He let me talk for a few minutes and then interrupted, "I don't do objectives, and I don't do performance appraisals. If any of my people have questions, they should see me." Then he looked at his watch to suggest our meeting was over. With a gulp, I responded, "Thank you for your time. I hope you will consider my suggestions," and I tried not to run as I left his office.

Once past the embarrassment of the exchange, I steadily coached the young vice president to initiate the objectives discussion himself, and he did so with moderate success. As a leader, his boss just disregarded that everyone, regardless of level, deserves a roadmap to understand how to succeed. The leader who consistently applies the basics, like Management 101, is providing that sought-after and needed map. The skills for leading effectively are the same whether you are managing many or few.

When a leader is entrusted with the work lives of other people, let alone five or six hundred people, that faith should be cause for reflection, a responsibility to be approached with a sense of humility rather than entitlement. Years ago, there was a video of a CEO who called himself a servant leader, who asserted that his job was to help his people be successful. He believed that the organization chart should be drawn bottom up, showing the workers at the top and the leader at the bottom, as the success of the organization depended on the success of his people. The video bore out that under his leadership with that ideal, the company was thriving. Servant leadership is an old concept going back to the sixth century BC in China, re-emerging in the Christian gospels and again in the 1970's. Servant leaders "consider themselves stewards" of the resources they manage, "and they give priority attention to the needs of their most important resource, their employees," per Wikipedia. They acknowledge that they need other people to be successful and in turn, they help them to succeed.

Rising in leadership, I worked very hard to apply these ideals and over time, shifted my efforts to helping people perform at their best. I began to let go and trust them to do their work, even if sometimes I kept my fingers crossed. When a leader does those things well, the team's accomplishments swell exponentially, and the leader is freed to do other things or to spend more time with those who actually need closer help.

Treat People with Authentic Interest and Respect

When I was in the Training and Development group in New York, I launched a new supervisory skills program entitled Interaction Management and went through a rigorous certification process. The program was composed of a series of pragmatic, how-to core modules that focused on the day-to-day interactions that all supervisors have with their employees. The program's fundamental themes: upholding the basic dignity of an individual, creating an environment where people can succeed, paying attention to the employee's self esteem and demonstrating empathy. That was my first educational experience in leadership, and I absorbed it like a sponge. Those were the skills that our supervisors and managers needed, skills I needed myself.

One of my bosses demonstrated how a genuine interest in people is indeed good business. He exhibited the same attentiveness when speaking to the cleaning people or those on the factory line as he did with peers and superiors. He was thoughtful in uncommon ways, earning him uncommon loyalty from those who worked with him. He knew about the people he came in contact with, along with the names of spouses; he remembered that a child had been sick or was excelling in school. He remembered because he was deeply interested. Other leaders switched on the caring behavior for the camera, but behind closed doors they slipped back to true character, very different from the public show. Such an act may work in the short term, but no one can keep it up endlessly, and over time employees see through the facade. My boss, though, consistently demonstrated unfeigned respect for people. Everyone could see his employees made the extra effort, not wanting to let him down. That is good business. The authentic, personal touch became important to me as a leader, and I worked hard to achieve it.

However, the road was not so easy, with my share of detours along the way. One regretful episode happened during my first assignment as Vice President, when I inherited the administrative assistant from my predecessor. My *admin* was having trouble keeping up with the rapid changes in workplace technology. Email was new, quickly taking over the business world, and she just could not acclimate in spite of attending repeated training programs. She was also quite disorganized, as evidenced by the stacks of papers on her desk, making it impossible to find a document that had yet to make it as far as the file cabinet.

I was forced to depend on her to manage the office while I was away on frequent business trips, handling a heavy flow of postal mail and email. As a result, she often missed essential information. We had discussions about the importance of improving her computer skills and the need to clean up her desk so we could find things. There was a marked lack of improvement in both areas.

My patience was depleted one weekend when I was in the office working on a project to be finished by Monday. I needed a document the admin would have filed, but it was nowhere, and I ended up searching through the piles on her desk with no luck. Frustrated, I did what I used to do at home when I saw disorder in my son's bedroom: I cleaned the mess myself. Then I put the piles on the floor beside a meticulously clean desk. Cooling down on the drive home, I knew my actions did not reflect good leadership and chastised myself the rest of the weekend. Granted we were mismatched, but I blew it. Come Monday morning, I headed for work feeling sick to my stomach. It felt worse when I saw how visibly upset the admin was. I had allowed my emotions to cloud my judgment, and my actions did not reflect respect for her as a human being. She was humiliated because the other admins saw what I had done. Given time to cool off, I could then have initiated the serious discussion calmly on Monday morning. We talked about the severity of the performance issues and ended up agreeing to part ways. Soon after, she left the company to join a small, low-tech family business.

The experience stayed with me the rest of my career, reminding me to treat people with respect and dignity regardless of the emotions of the moment. I worked on being approachable and genuine; on establishing a personal connection with people. And with time I made progress. Personal integrity comes into play here, too. There were times when my next meeting was with the perennial complainer, and it would have been too easy to either deny him the meeting or coast through it. But I took the time to focus on him and listen to what he had to say. To be true to my job, I had to put aside my feelings and pay attention, because maybe that time the issue was serious.

Our behaviors are shaped by our assumptions, which fill in because we cannot know it all. We make assumptions about people's intent and thereby affect how they respond to us in turn. When I suspected other people of negative intent, I found it helpful to flip things around and consider at least one positive assumption. What else might they have meant? Why not assume good intentions could be at play? Most people mean well and want to do well for the organization and for themselves. It is natural that if you have respect for people, you accept that good people can make bad decisions. One of the most compelling and gifted leaders in my career, who courageously stood by the truth, taught me this: "Assume positive intent." She had tremendous emotional maturity and truly cared about the underdog. That kind of wisdom drew enormous affinity for the way she chose to live out her work life.

Spread Self-Confidence Around

A number of years ago at a luncheon, former New York City Mayor Rudolph Giuliani spoke about leadership. He said if a leader "doesn't believe" he will succeed, the sourness becomes a self-fulfilling prophecy. Confidence in a leader is energizing and enabling all around. Giuliani's perspective resonated with me, always more receptive to a leader who believed in himself. When he was confident, I was confident. My teammates also responded positively and were more willing to stretch for the big wins. A confident leader is also upbeat and capable of painting a picture of what success looks like, even excited about believing he can do it. People respond positively—they want to be on his team and they trust more in their own ability to succeed.

Together with positive energy, one quality that stands out in a highly confident leader is a deep knowledge base in his field. For one period of the least profitable unit in my company, our business was constantly rumored to be for sale, and that is when the contagious enthusiasm of good leadership played out on a broader scale. As leaders of this business, we worked very hard to emphasize the positives of being the smallest unit: everyone knew everyone else; organizational politics played less of a factor in decision making; we had the benefits of a small company with the resources of a large corporation. Finding the silver lining in every cloud became an important leadership quality if we were to inject energy into the unit.

A leader is not intimidated by big challenges, because he trusts his ability to respond to the unforeseen. The leader who was appointed to run our small unit had spent his career in the industry, and he spoke with conviction about the issues affecting the business. He acknowledged the difficulties and showed how to overcome them in a way the workers and senior leadership could also envision. Just as he was able to project his belief that we could turn the business around, we proceeded to make unprecedented changes in core aspects of the business. The boost of energy in the organization was palpable, and we succeeded.

Learn From Your Experiences—Positive and Negative

The best leaders do not beat themselves up when plans fall through. Failures cannot erode their confidence, because when leaders lose confidence, the organization also loses confidence. When they hit a tough spot, successful leaders revisit their goals, engage their followers and move in a new direction to achieve the goal. Beneath it all, they rely on fundamental confidence and optimism.

One such inspiring leader is an Anglican priest in the interior of Panama, a quiet man, comfortable with himself and confident in his mission. He ministers to seven small parishes, some so remote that in the rainy season he must travel on horseback. The needs vary from replacing a leaky old roof to rebuilding a church on higher ground due to repeated flooding when the nearby river crests. Father Heladio spoke of how overwhelmed and defeated the parishioners felt by these seemingly insurmountable challenges. Yet, only a few months after *El Padre* was appointed, he helped them organize a fund raiser that netted them $1,700, or 10% of the cost to replace the leaky roof. When the parishioners worried about the remaining 90%, El Padre patiently pointed out that $1,700 is more than they had the previous year. His deep faith, read optimism, inspired the parishioners to work harder to make more happen. Generating one small win and a good dose of infectious optimism, he energized his parishioners to undertake the impossible. Padre Heladio's unique qualities motivated a traveling group to join his campaign, and he currently has both major projects under way.

There are leaders who walk around with a dark cloud over their heads, inspiring anything but confidence. They tend to miss the powerful impact of a vision of hope. How much more could they accomplish if they were able to inspire awe in the most difficult of circumstances? Let's not underestimate the capacity of individuals with vision to do great things, to surpass overwhelming challenges and to fulfill improbable dreams. They can do those things because of the intangible qualities of confidence and optimism. Optimism fuels confidence. Together they are a powerful force towards achieving a goal that might otherwise seem beyond reach.

UPON REFLECTION,
here are some takeaways to
Leadership:

A leader's job is to help others perform at their best
for the benefit of the business.

Respect for people is fundamental to great leadership: honor the basic
dignity of the individual, create an environment for success, pay
attention to self esteem and demonstrate empathy.

Confidence and optimism are a powerful combination in a leader.
Silver lining, dark cloud—your choice.

Part Nine

Generosity

The Responsibility to Give Back

We honor those who contributed to our success
by doing the same for others.

I am the beneficiary of the American experience, a giving society. I was given a chance at success—from government assistance to a four-year scholarship to many individual mentors and sponsors. Benefiting from such good fortune, I feel a sense of responsibility to give back in the same way. Yet the impact today of receiving so much is no obligation at all, but the passion to reciprocate by bestowing the same gifts on others. Generosity breeds generosity.

Mentor and Sponsor

Much of the success I met can be attributed to what special

individuals granted me—permission—those keys of confidence that freed me to move beyond barriers and think beyond my dreams. The high school teacher who pointed me towards Barnard College, the professor who picked me out of an ASPIRA meeting to teach undergraduates, the pharmaceutical leader who guided me through a change in career and the leaders who took chances on me all impacted my life dramatically. Each had contributed to my evolving vision of what was possible, the much-appreciated keys. To help others in the same way, I became drawn to mentoring. I paid particular attention to the young people, women and minorities looking for guidance on how to succeed in a large and complex organization. If I could touch even one person in the way I was touched with insight and kindness, I could start sharing my passion to reciprocate.

Mentoring, as opposed to tutoring, is helping people think through decisions, being a model for them, sharing a few secrets and only sometimes showing them how to perform tasks. The best mentors ask good questions and are even better as listeners. They focus on understanding the goals of their 'mentee,' and instead of dispensing wise answers, mentors focus on the process of helping people reach their own conclusions.

The best mentees know what they want out of the process, and they take responsibility for managing the relationship. One formal mentoring program paired me for one full year with a promising young man from another business unit. As I prepared for my first meeting with him, I was concerned. Mentoring was different from coaching day-to-day, because my mentee was in a distant unit of the company. Never having observed him at work, I had to apply my listening skills and the insights from experience. Clever mentee, he made it easy by showing up at our meetings prepared with specific subjects, experiences or theoretical situations he wanted to discuss. As I shared similar accounts, my mentee reached his own conclusions as a result of the exchange. Not only did my thoughts help him, analyzing them also helped me gain a deeper understanding of myself. By extracting lessons from my own experiences, I was growing as a leader. What worked, what went wrong and why? What could I have done differently? Thinking through stories was making them more valuable to me and others. We both enjoyed a special relationship that continued beyond the official mentoring year.

Affinity groups present another satisfying way to mentor young people at work. Participating in a Hispanic group, junior members who were hungry for insights to success could interact with senior Hispanics in the organization and extract lessons from their personal accounts. We were all appreciative of a forum for sharing our experiences as Hispanics.

At larger groups, too, people were indeed interested in personal accounts, especially coping with the challenges of single motherhood and career, balancing personal life with work life and dealing with discrimination face to face. After I spoke at a conference, a young woman came up and confided how overwhelmed she felt by the pressures of marriage, a child, a job and school. She had been thinking of dropping out of school, but now more encouraged, she decided to stay in school. How cool is that? She would do it, but had to figure out how. Her renewed zeal then reinforced how much I valued giving back.

Many of my mentors were also sponsors. Sponsoring goes beyond teaching, sharing experiences and modeling behavior. A sponsor, affectionately called angel or rabbi, is someone who has a high opinion of you and is proactive about giving you the experience and exposure that will help move you up the organization. Because they are usually at a high level in the organization, they have relationships to tap into and get other leaders to notice you. As a result, you may be offered opportunities sooner than you might have on your own.

I benefited from many sponsors in my career. One leader could get air time with the senior leaders, and during his meetings he would talk about his best people. He was not fearful of losing choice staff to other parts of the organization. He helped his talented people move on, although it meant retraining others to fill vacant positions. He used his diversified portfolio of relationships to introduce me to senior leaders I otherwise would never have met. My high school teacher played the double role of mentor and sponsor. As a mentor, he kept an eye on me during the school year and was there for me if I did poorly on an exam. As an active sponsor who encouraged me to apply to Barnard, he then phoned to talk to the woman in Admissions who would be interviewing me there. These are the kinds of mentors and sponsors that make a great difference in people's lives.

"A rising tide lifts all boats," said President John F. Kennedy. Regardless of where you work, what you do, where you come from and what your race or ethnicity is, you can support and help each other. Help the tide rise. No matter how much of a beginner you may be, the next level is higher—and so, sponsoring should be active along the many levels of the organization. From supervisor to manager, manager to director, director to vice president, it is a selfless act, because when you move the talent along, that talent must leave your group. Yet you will experience the satisfaction of watching them grow as they move on to bigger challenges, and of watching your reputation as a leader rise with that tide.

Give Back to the Community

Philanthropy is integral to American life, where a large percent of the population gives generously to those in need. The land of opportunity that made it possible for a sugar cane plantation girl to be ushered into the boardroom of one of the largest companies in the world cannot provide directly for everyone in need. Our social system depends on individual patronage to supplement official efforts. My years in a company that valued the communities where our employees lived and worked reinforced my sense of social responsibility. And so I applaud volunteering, philanthropy and the many other ways people contribute to the wellbeing of others.

When I could give back financially, I focused first on my family, helping the next generation stay in school. Later, I started giving back to Barnard College through a scholarship fund named after my parents, in honor of their focus on education. I give back to my old neighborhood through membership on the Board of Grand Street Settlement, an exceptional non-profit organization that provides services to the neediest people in the Lower East Side.

This book is another way of giving back, with the hope that a broader audience is inspired by the personal accounts and my take on what they mean. If only one person's life is changed for the better, then at least some of the dream of reciprocating is fulfilled.

Go Beyond
the Dreams

There are many paths that go forward.

Reviewing my life and articulating what I learned had social implications beyond the lessons of what helps and hinders success, my original intent. Far from disadvantaged, my siblings and I were blessedly advantaged—to have parents who were ever-present in our lives. Their hard work, tough love, and above-all-odds belief in us lit the spark that later evolved into self confidence and the tenacity to work through hard times. These were the qualities that brought me to the boardroom. And as every good tale has a hero, I cede that role happily to my parents, the rightful heroes of the story.

We have a responsibility to the next generation to provide a strong and supportive family unit. The best home does not have to be a conventional home as long as it is an affirming environment—guiding the development of values and the learning experience. Our parents may not have been able to help us with our schoolwork, but they made quiet time for it. They reviewed our report cards and attended parent-teacher meetings. There was no doubt in our family that school was primary and that our parents cared. Send your family the same message loud and clear.

While parental life may be easier if you share it with a partner, a single parent can also provide a healthy home for her children as long as there is love, support and good role models of extended family and friends. Note that a broken home is not by definition one of divorce. A broken home may appear to be intact, yet dysfunctional or always angry. Better a peaceful divorce. Divorce is not the cause, but the result of, an already broken home.

Focus on What You Can Control

Always maintain forward momentum, especially after a stumble. When my marriage ended, I moved on. When I faced discrimination, I worked to prove the bias wrong. When I failed a major exam, I studied harder. When my career slowed down, I continued to give my best anyway. To overcome the fear of public speaking, I kept putting myself in front of groups. Each time, I focused on what I could control, directing my energy towards the many paths that could drive the wheels forward.

Stuck in neutral or splattered in mud, the one thing you most definitely control is how you act when it hits the fan. While there are situations that can lead us to react without thinking and make the wrong choices, we actively choose how we respond to the people and circumstances in our lives. Rather than reacting, I recommend choosing a path that keeps you progressing towards your goal.

Round the Full Circle of Valuing Who and What You Are

As I approached the age when one prudently plans for retirement, I wondered how easy that transition to a happy retiree would be. When the day did come, I plunged in the only way I know how, with energy and optimism. After 32 years as a bachelorette and 18 years of courting, I married my best friend, so my first year as a retiree was filled with wedding plans, home construction and relocating. In researching retirement, I was drawn to Ernie J. Zelinski's book *How to Retire Happy, Wild, and Free*. Zelinski says that individuals who tie their self-worth exclusively to their work could have trouble in retirement without the activity that gives them a sense of value. Bingo! The message fit like a bull's-eye within my mantra "Value who and what you are." When your sense of self comes from within, you carry it with you no matter where life takes you. The early experiences that taught me to value self were fundamental, not only to career success but most importantly, to a fulfilling life.

Three years into my retirement, I have yet to look back. The morning workouts at the gym are still an important part of the day, and I enjoy the freedom to do things I had simply put aside because of work: making friends in a new community, spending more time with the grandkids, expanding my role in the non-profit work, sipping *café con leche* mornings with Mom, cooking for guests and having the very satisfying experience of being owned by our dog, Max.

Most remarkable of all was becoming an author. Writing a book was never in my dreams, never a possibility. And yet here I am, in my sixtieth year, daring to say I have tales to tell that you may be interested in reading.

On the day of my final promotion, I reflected on the road that brought me up from a house on stilts to the top-floor boardroom of a top-tier global company. I felt a sense of urgency towards the nearly 100,000 colleagues around the world I would be privileged to represent, plus profound gratitude for the leaders who believed in me. I would not let them down. Success in a role beyond my dreams would demand drawing upon every bit of wisdom acquired along the way. That great day in the boardroom, I had indeed gone beyond my dreams, but the biggest lesson was yet to come as I continued the journey into retirement. I plunged into retirement with the modest hope of being a happy retiree and found much more—a great adventure with beginnings, not endings, and more energizing challenges. There is no end to learning and no end to the possibilities this life offers.

Upon reflection

1. Believe in yourself.

Fundamental to every success story is belief in oneself; a strong sense of self engenders optimism and an orientation to action – a powerful combination.

2. Always take responsibility for your actions, including mistakes.

The candid reality is that one must be accountable for individual performance. Be proactive about your own learning and face challenges with tenacity.

3. Listen carefully and present yourself carefully.

Beyond performance, organizational savvy and meticulous presentation of self are essential for career success.

4. Succeed by creating success around you.

Leadership is all about helping others perform and then letting go. A deep respect for people is at the core of great leadership.

5. Take charge.

You are in control of your actions. Respond constructively to adversity, building relationships in ways that continue the forward momentum.

Made in the USA
Lexington, KY
23 September 2011